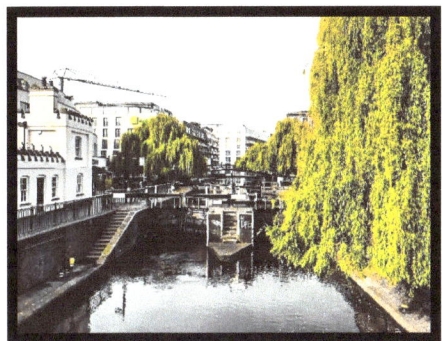

Colour London

By

Karry Weather

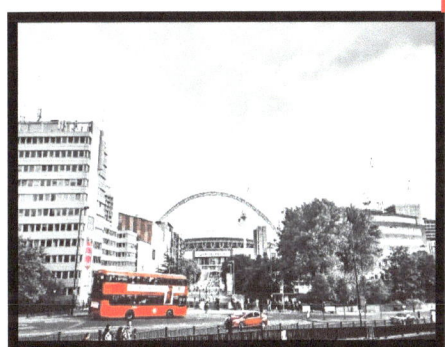
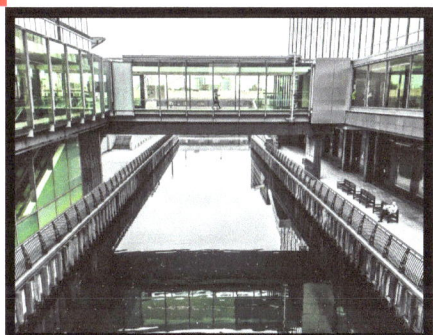

Printed in 2017

Text, images and photographs produced by Karry Weather.

No part of this publication may be reproduced or transmitted in any form whatsoever without prior permission obtained in writing.

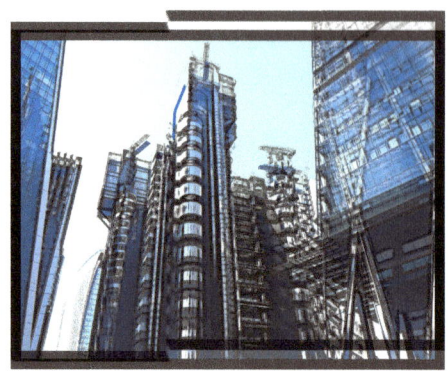
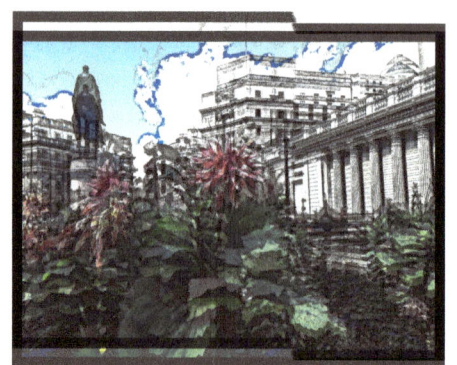

Think London, and most people think red. The stunning red of the London Routemaster bus, the pillar boxes, red since as early as 1884, the telephone booths and Underground roundels are complemented by the uniforms of the Chelsea Pensioners, Tower of London Beefeaters and the Royal Guards. However, London is also a green city with many famous parks, avenues of trees and tranquil garden squares. Of course the traditional black cabs and the shiny black paint of 10 Downing Street are equally iconic, whilst the newer glass buildings at the centre of London's two financial hubs reflect the blueness of the Thames. This book encourages you to explore and enjoy colouring the different shades and tints of this vibrant city as you let your imagination run wild and explore its history.

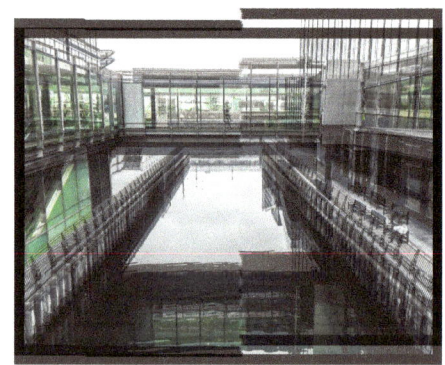
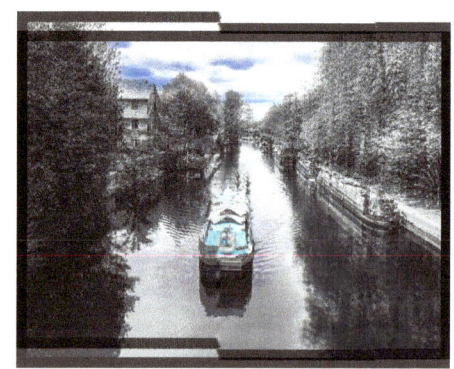

When a man is tired of London, he is tired of life.

Samuel Johnson.

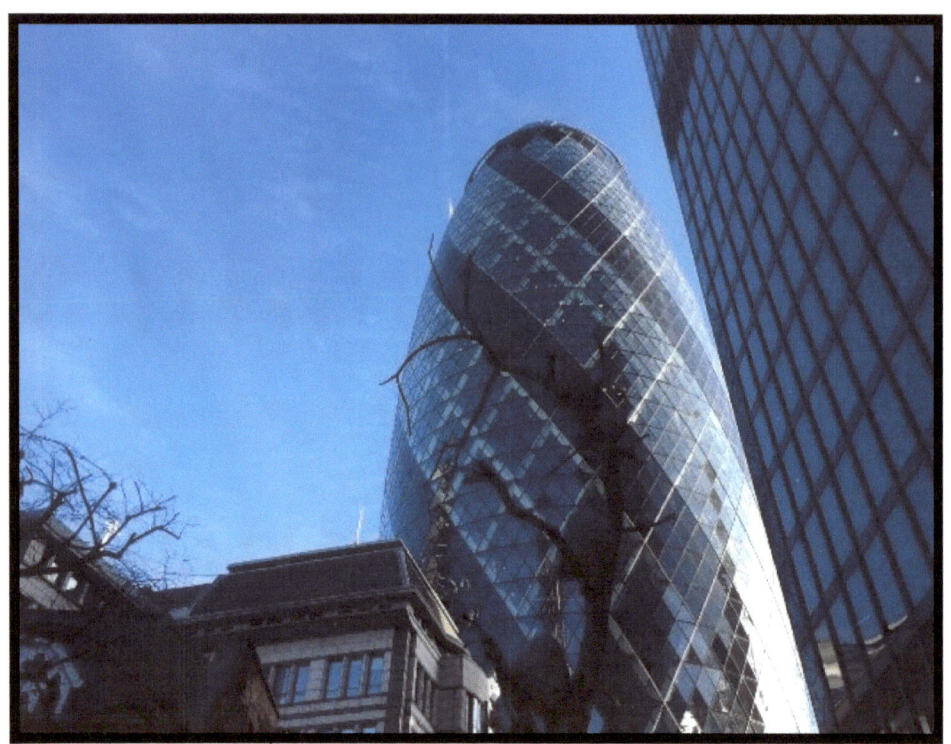

LONDON EC3A 8EP

Londoners like to give their buildings a nickname and 30 St Mary Axe is better known as the Gherkin. It is 180m high with 41 floors. It opened in April 2004 and is a skyscraper in the financial centre of the square mile. It is one of London's most instantly recognisable landmarks. It is built on the former sites of the Baltic Exchange and Chamber of Shipping. It is a short walk from both Liverpool Street Tube Station and Aldgate Tube Station. It houses an elegant restaurant, bar and street food outlets. Although not normally open to the public, it can be accessed during Open House London which is always a popular event. It has featured in a number of films including 'Harry Potter and the Half Blood Prince'. Designed by Sir Norman Foster its curves of light and dark glass are both distinctive and eye catching. Enjoy colouring.

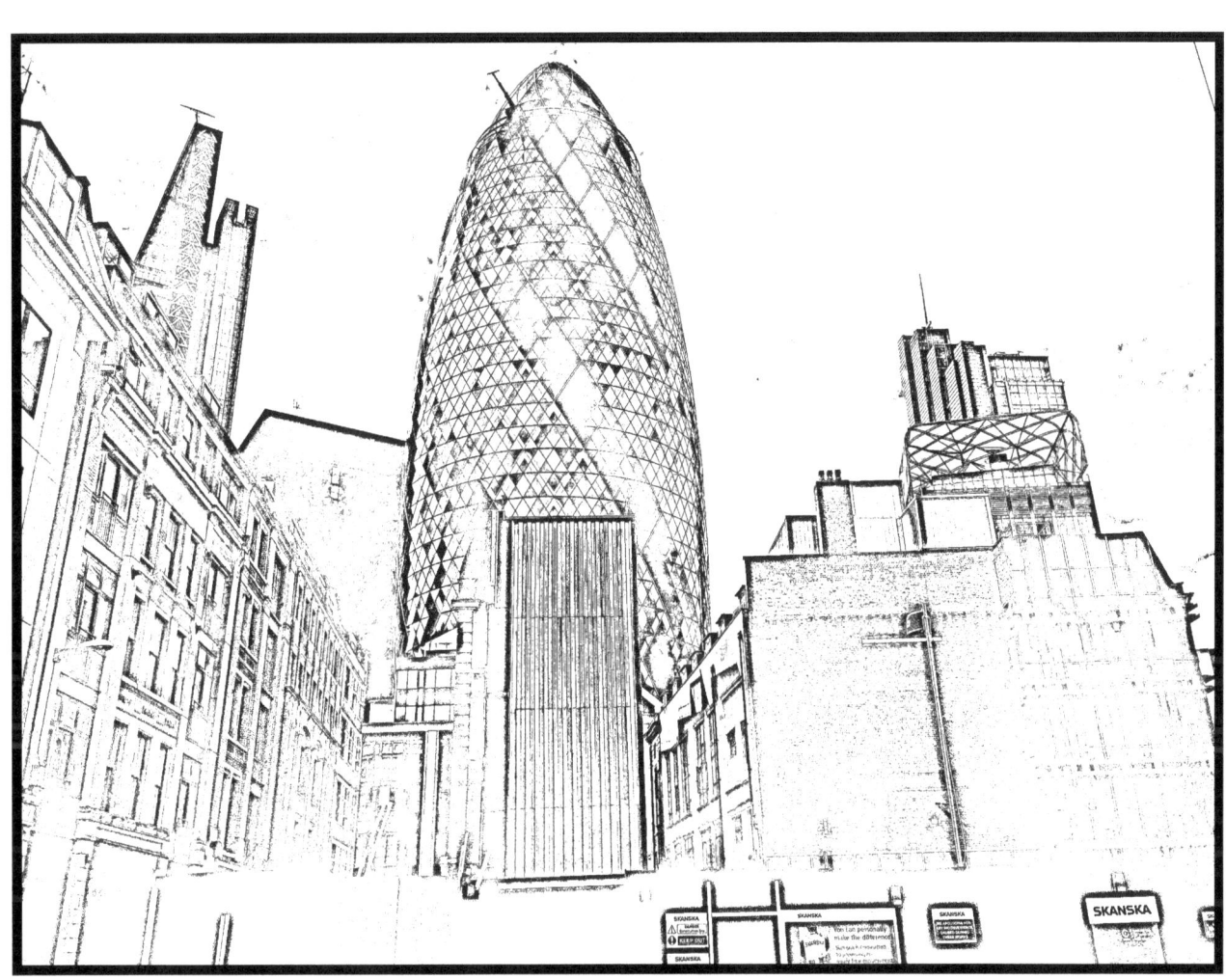

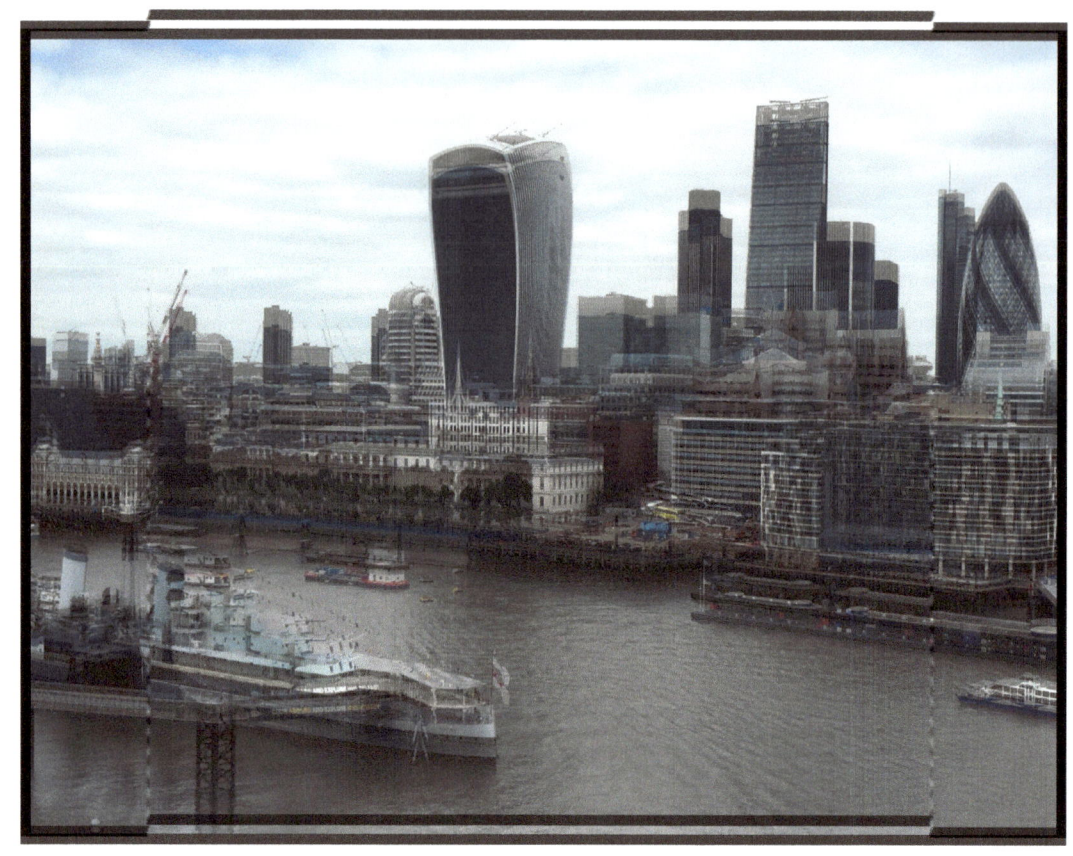

The City of London is known as the Square Mile and contains the primary business area of London and its historic centre. It is unclear exactly when London was founded but possibly as early as 43AD. The Romans developed it as a port but it was destroyed by Boudica in 60 AD. It was rebuilt as a walled settlement and ultimately replaced Camulodunum (Colchester) as the capital. Alfred the Great, the first King of England, occupied the area around 886AD William the Conqueror subsequently built three castles, one of which, The Tower of London, still stands. Many of the new buildings and landmarks that form the City nowadays are popularly given a nickname e.g. The Walkie Talkie, blamed for melting cars; the Leadenhall Building, called the Cheesegrater because of its distinctive wedge shape; and, 110 Bishopsgate unofficially called the Heron Tower. Enjoy colouring.

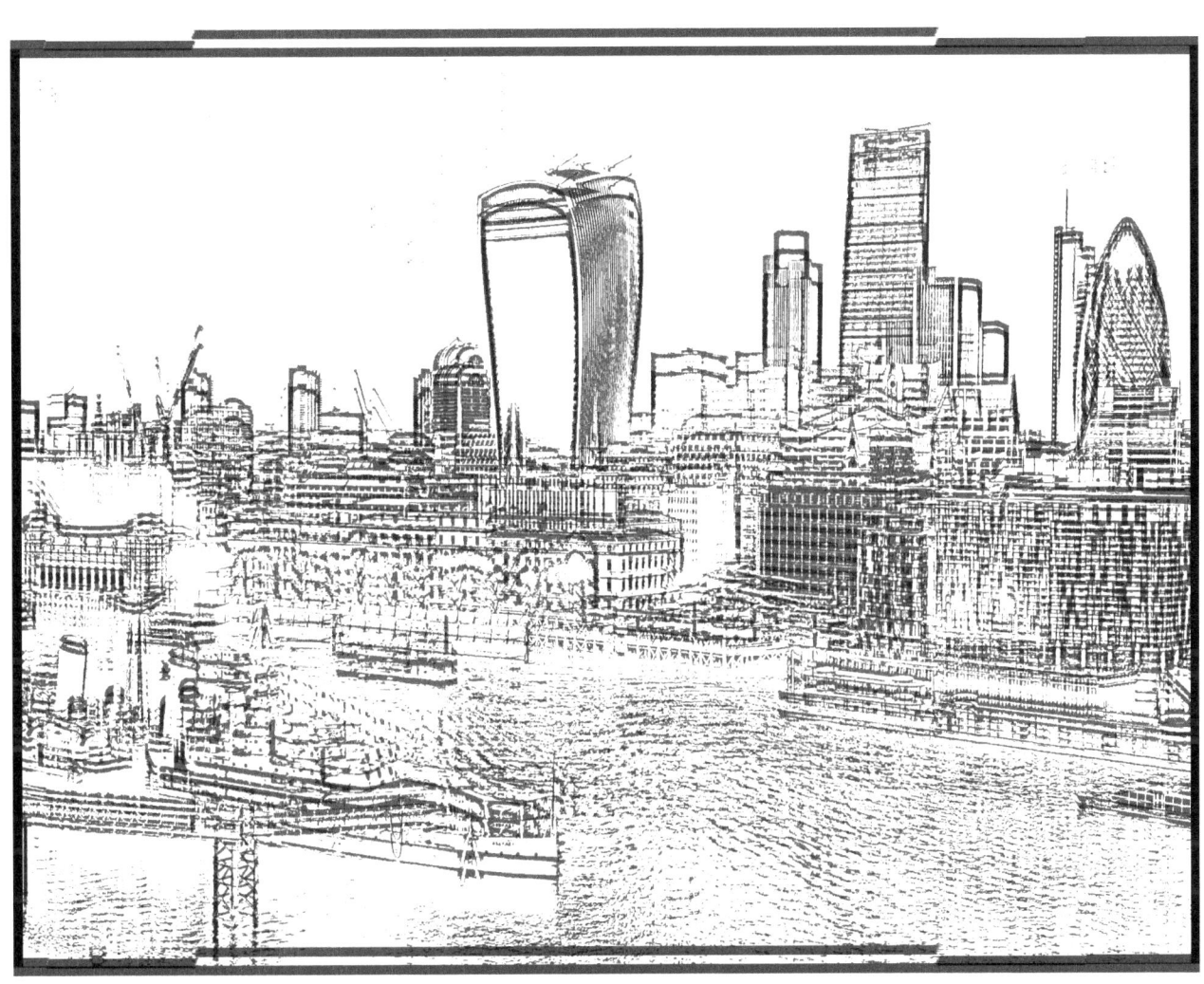

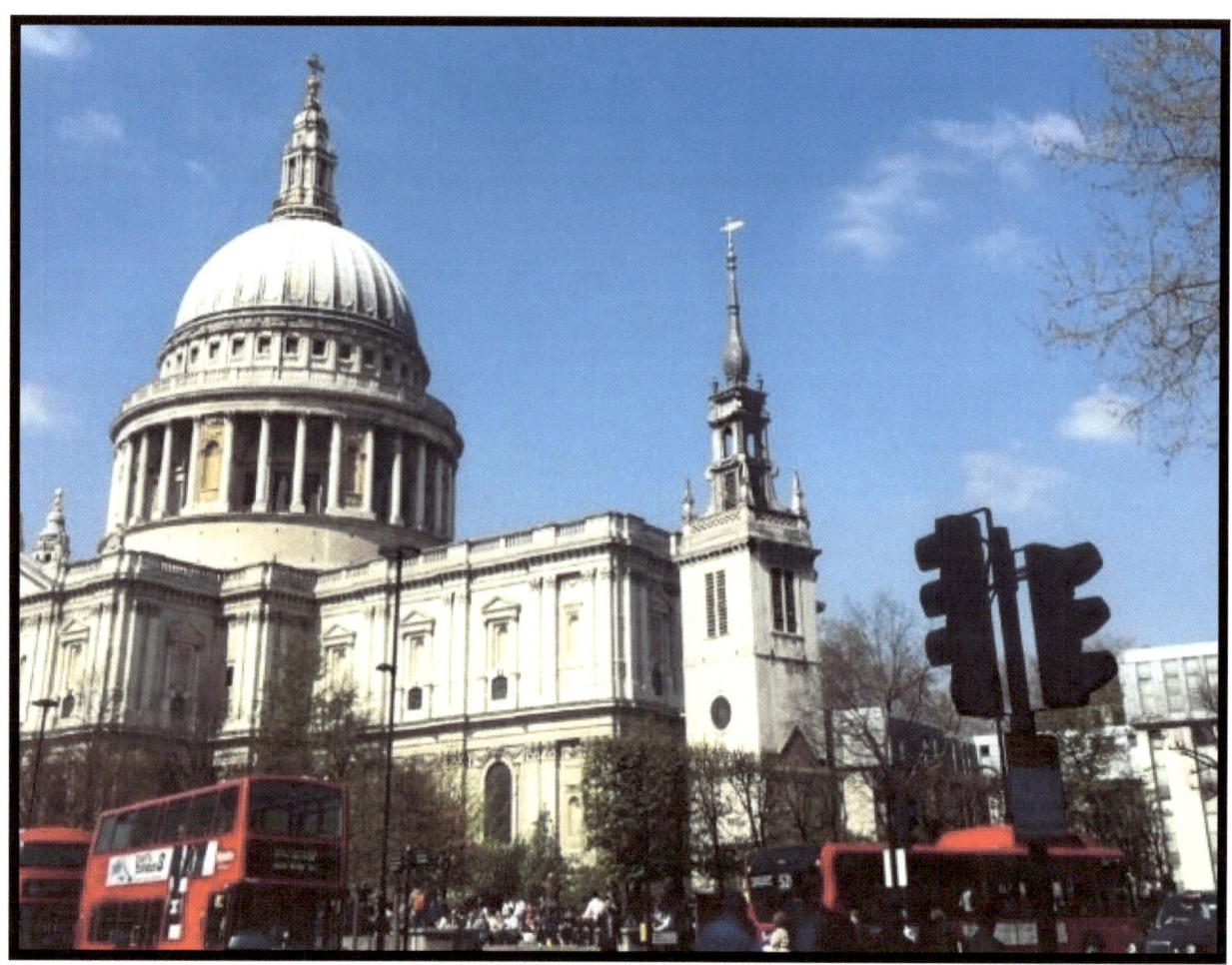

London EC4M 8AD

St. Paul's Cathedral is the seat of the Bishop of London, dedicated to Paul the Apostle. The original medieval church founded in 604AD was destroyed in the Great Fire of London. The present day cathedral was designed by Sir Christopher Wren. The cathedral has played a significant part in the history of London. Weddings held here include the marriage of Prince Charles to Lady Diana Spencer and funerals include Sir Winston Churchill's and Baroness Margaret Thatcher. It is a working church, free to worshippers, but there is a fee for tourists. The nearest tube stations are St. Paul's, Mansion House and Blackfriars. Enjoy colouring

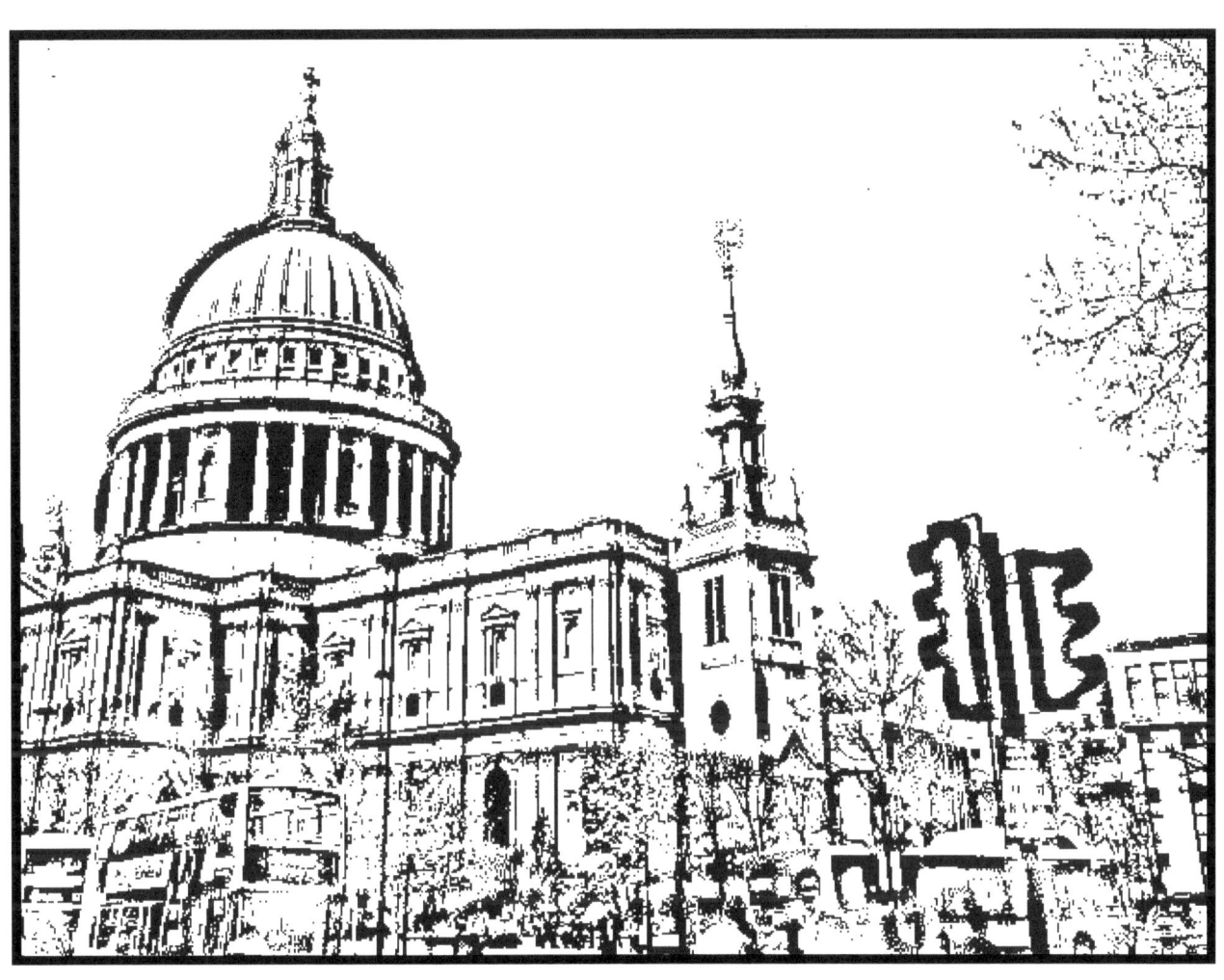

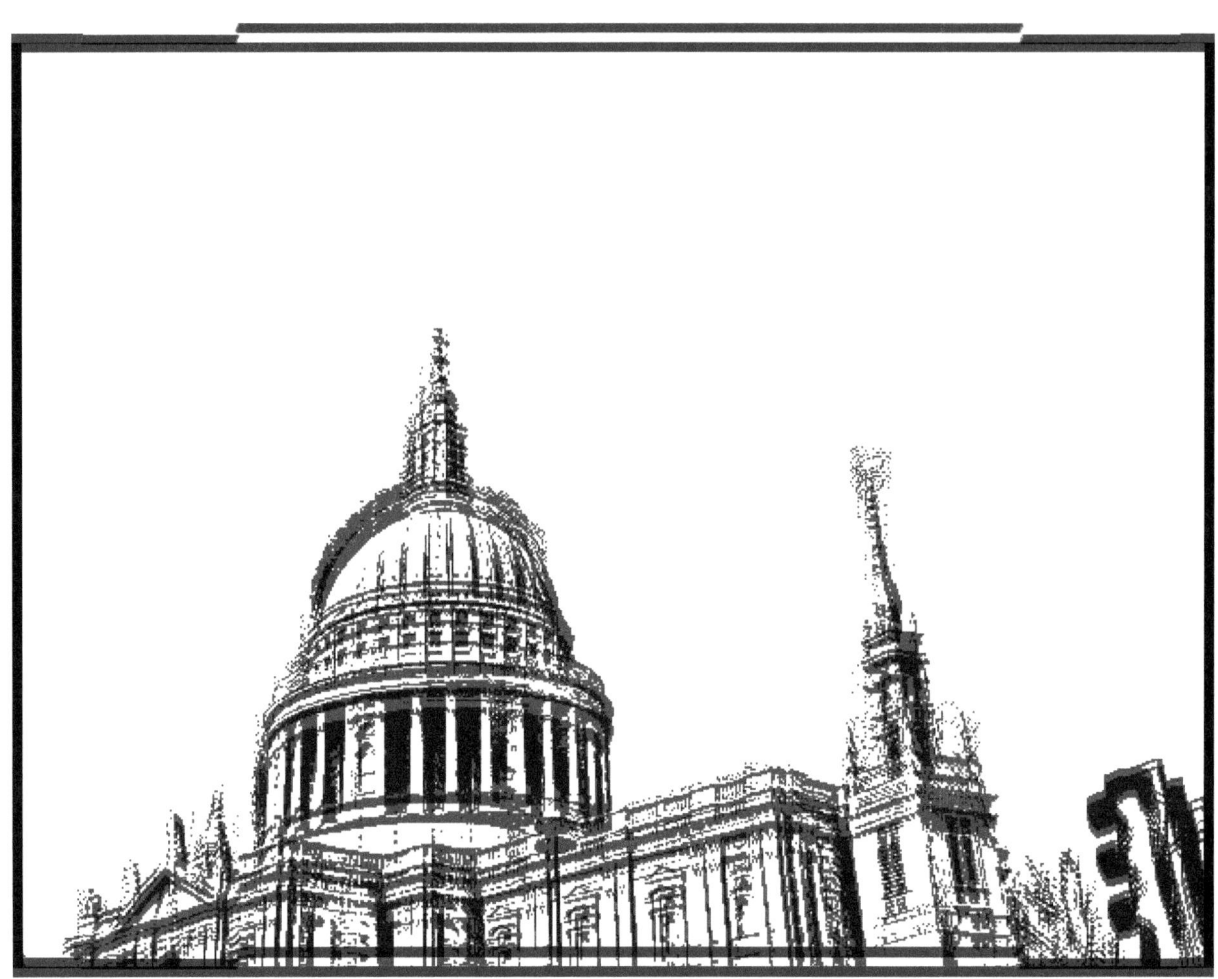

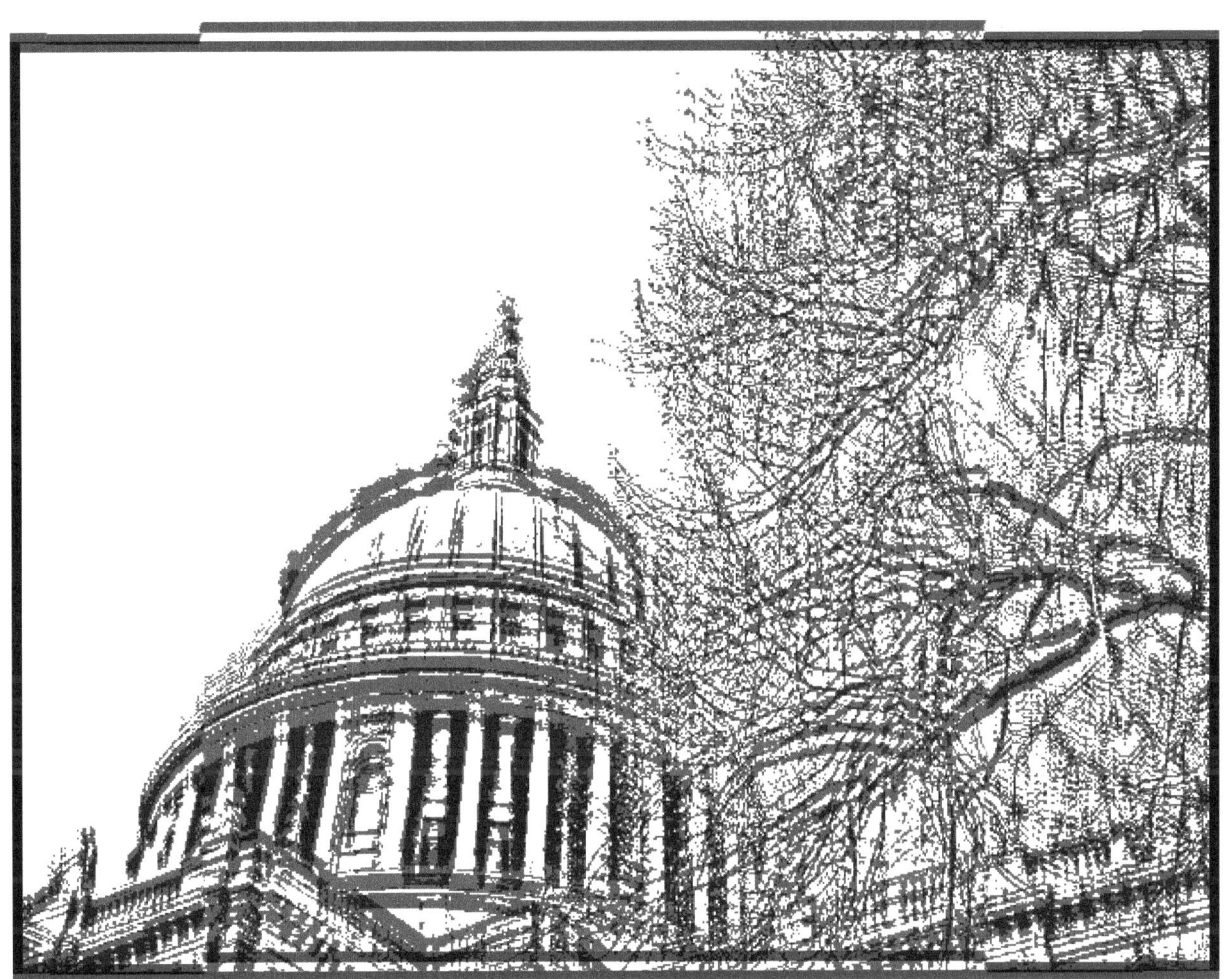

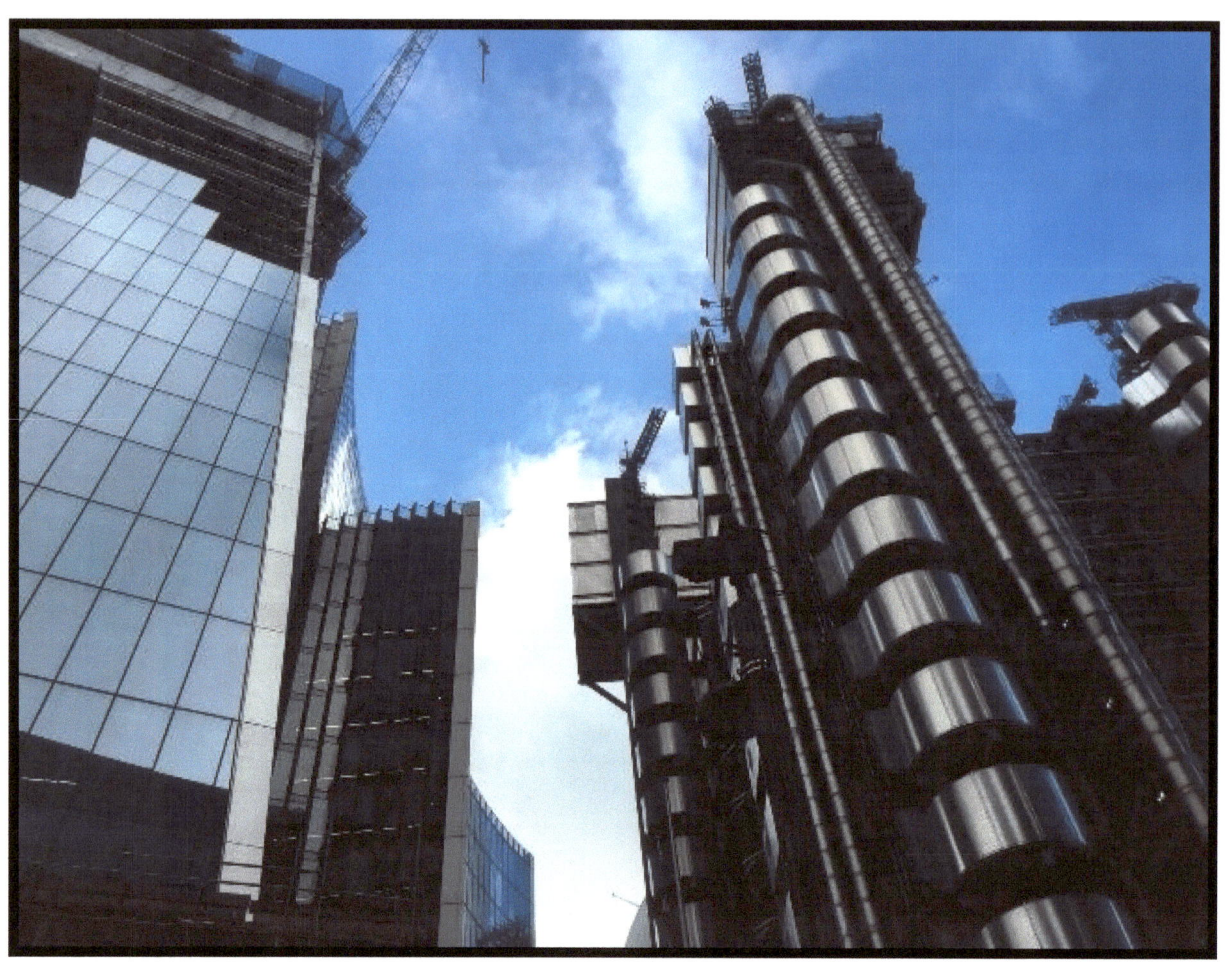

London EC3M 7HA

The Lloyds building houses a world famous insurance market consisting of financial backers many of whom are corporations and some private individuals called 'Names'. It was founded by Edward Lloyd initially to cover marine insurance. It is over 300 years old and acts as a market regulator. It is the oldest insurance marketplace in the world. The closest tube stations are Monument, Bank and Aldgate. Take a leisurely stroll around the City streets and soak up the atmosphere and history of the Square Mile. Enjoy colouring.

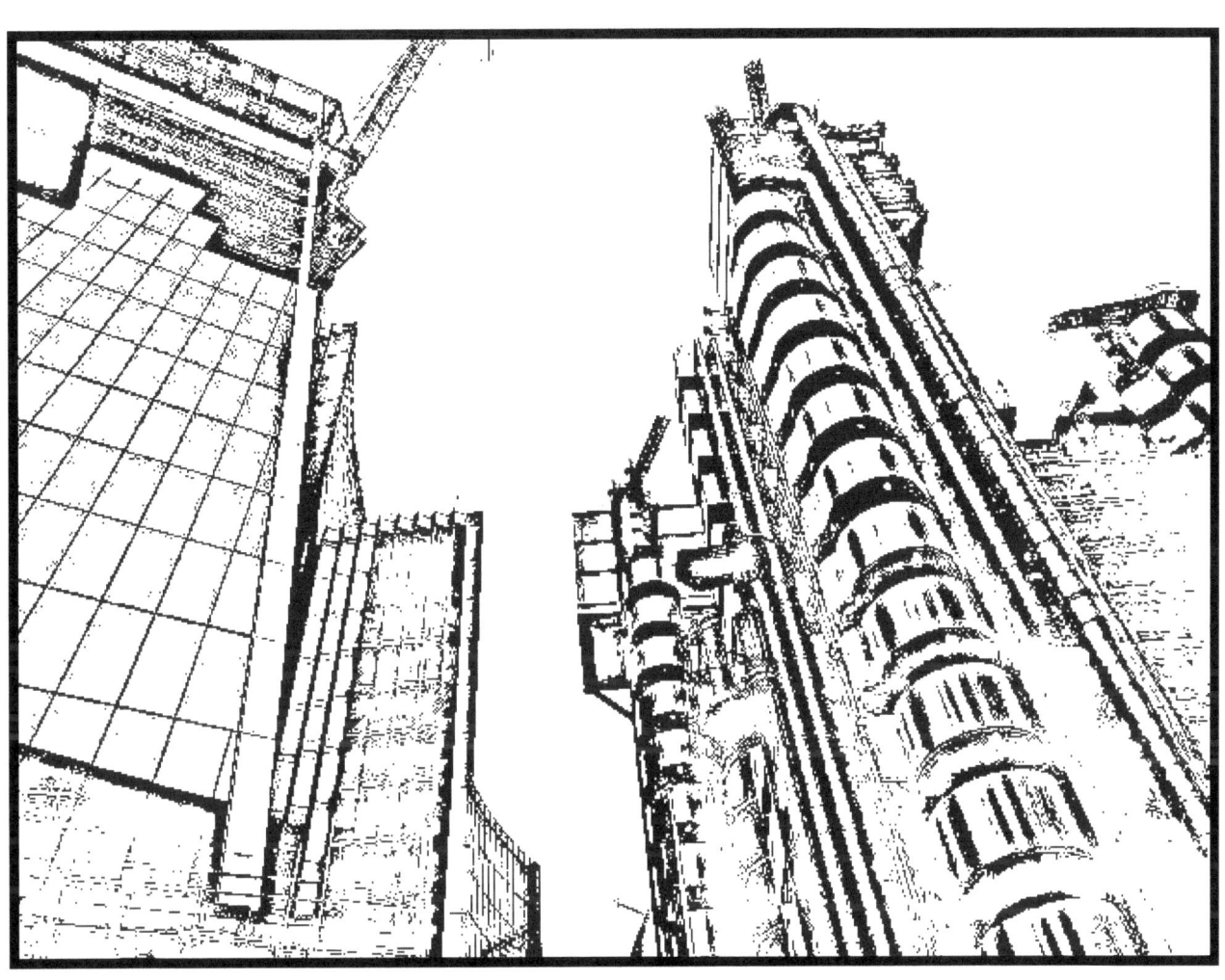

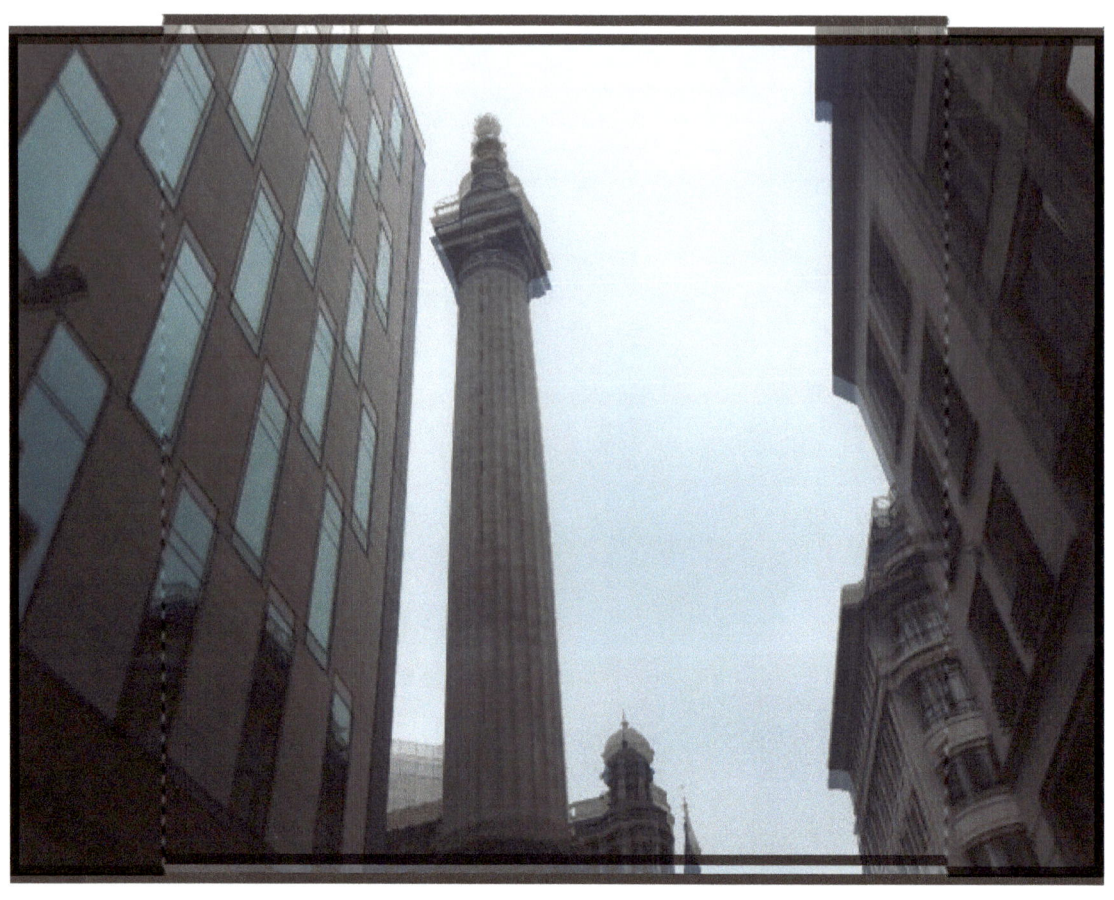

London EC3R 8AH

In 1665, London suffered a major epidemic of bubonic plague, called the Great Plague, killing about one quarter of the population. Much of the City was then lost in 1666 in The Great Fire of London which destroyed most of the old medieval City over three days following a long, hot summer. The fire is often credited with having halted the plague and the nursery rhyme 'London's Burning' is said to be about The Great Fire. The fire began in the early morning of Sunday 2nd September in a bakery owned by a Thomas Faryner on Pudding Lane. Most of the City was built of timber with crowded houses and narrow streets so the fire spread rapidly. Personal accounts of the spread of the fire can be read in Samuel Pepys diary. The Monument to the Great Fire of London, more simply known as the Monument was designed by Sir Christopher Wren and stands 62 metres high and 62 metres from where the fire started in Pudding Lane. The nearest tube stations are Monument and London Bridge. Enjoy colouring.

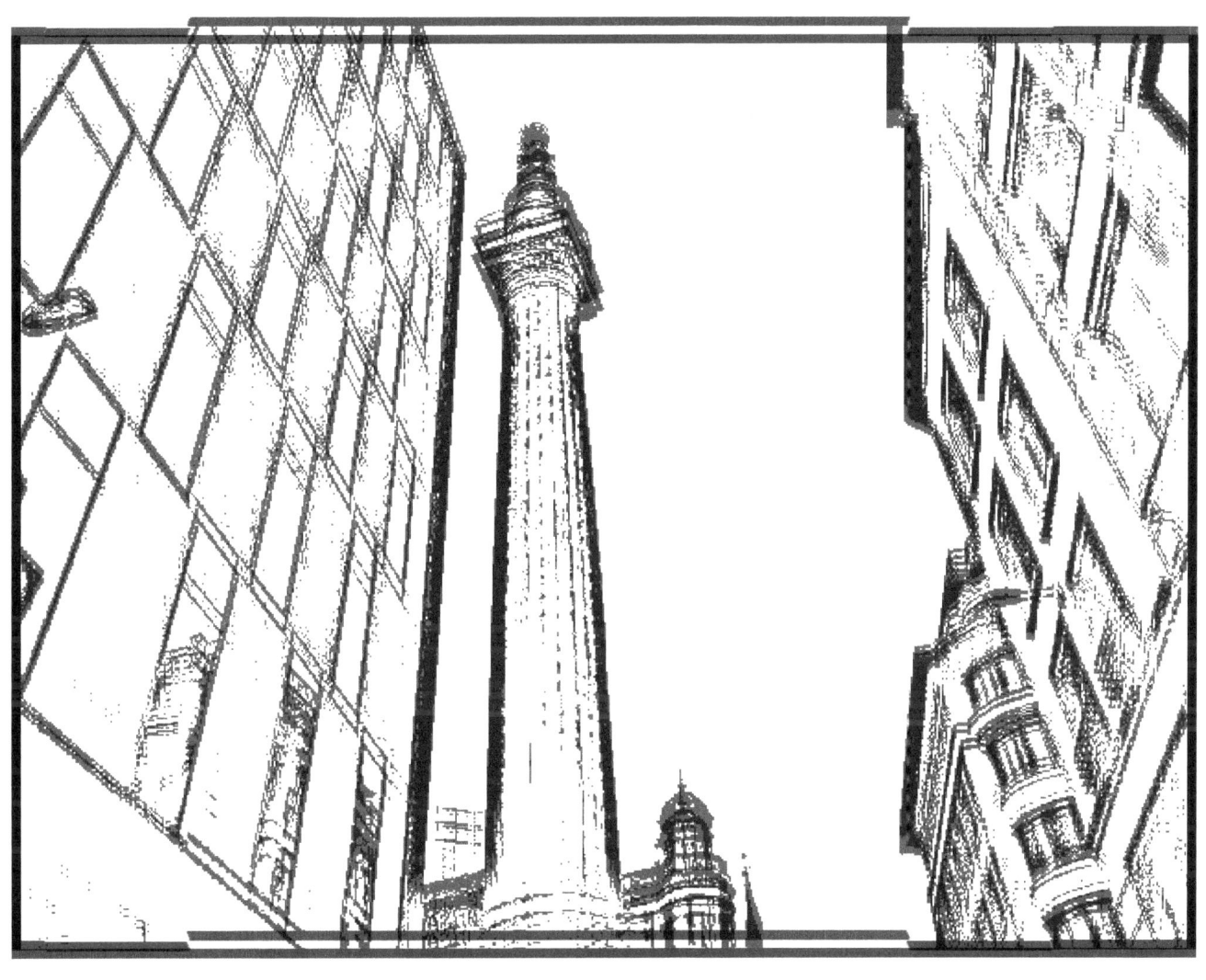

The churches, houses and all on fire and flaming at once.

Samuel Pepys diary.

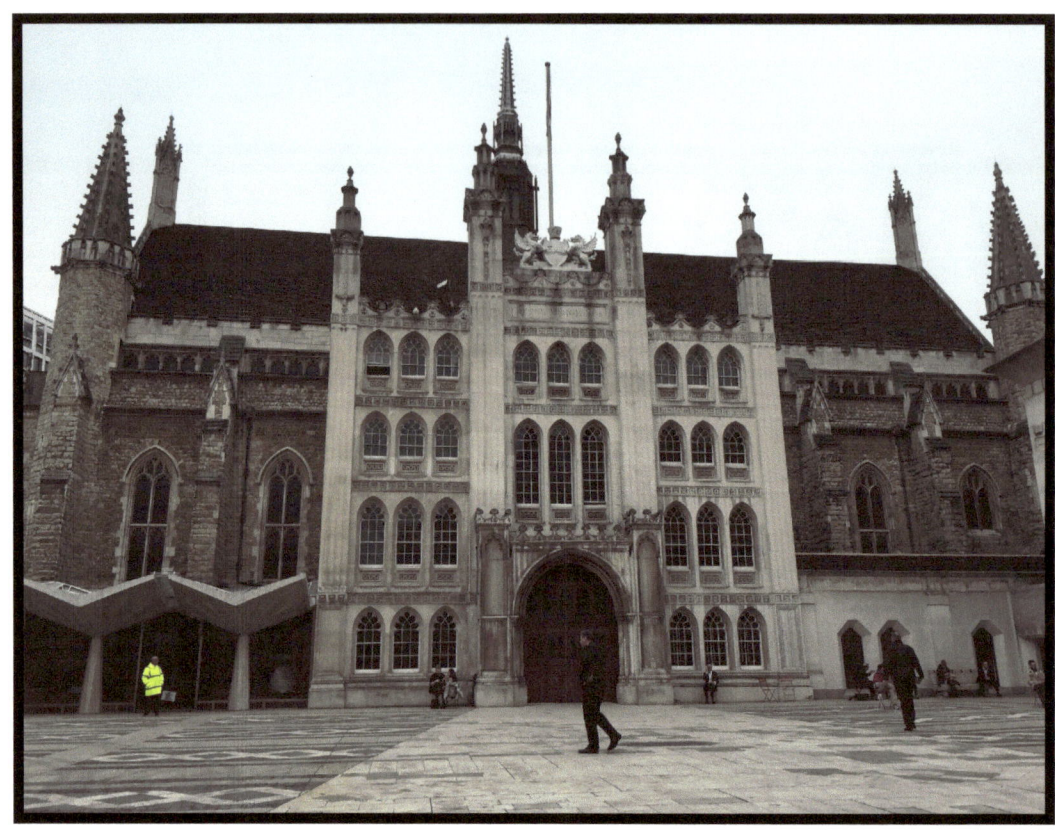

London EC2V 7HH

Guildhall houses a medieval great hall. Trials in this hall have included those of Thomas Culpepper, Lady Jane Grey and Thomas Cranmer to name but a few. It contains memorials to Lord Nelson, Sir Winston Churchill and both Pitt the Younger and Elder. Guildhall is used for official functions nowadays, most famously, the Lord Mayor's Banquet and is open to the public during London Open House events. The nearest tube stations are Bank, Moorgate and St. Paul's. Enjoy colouring.

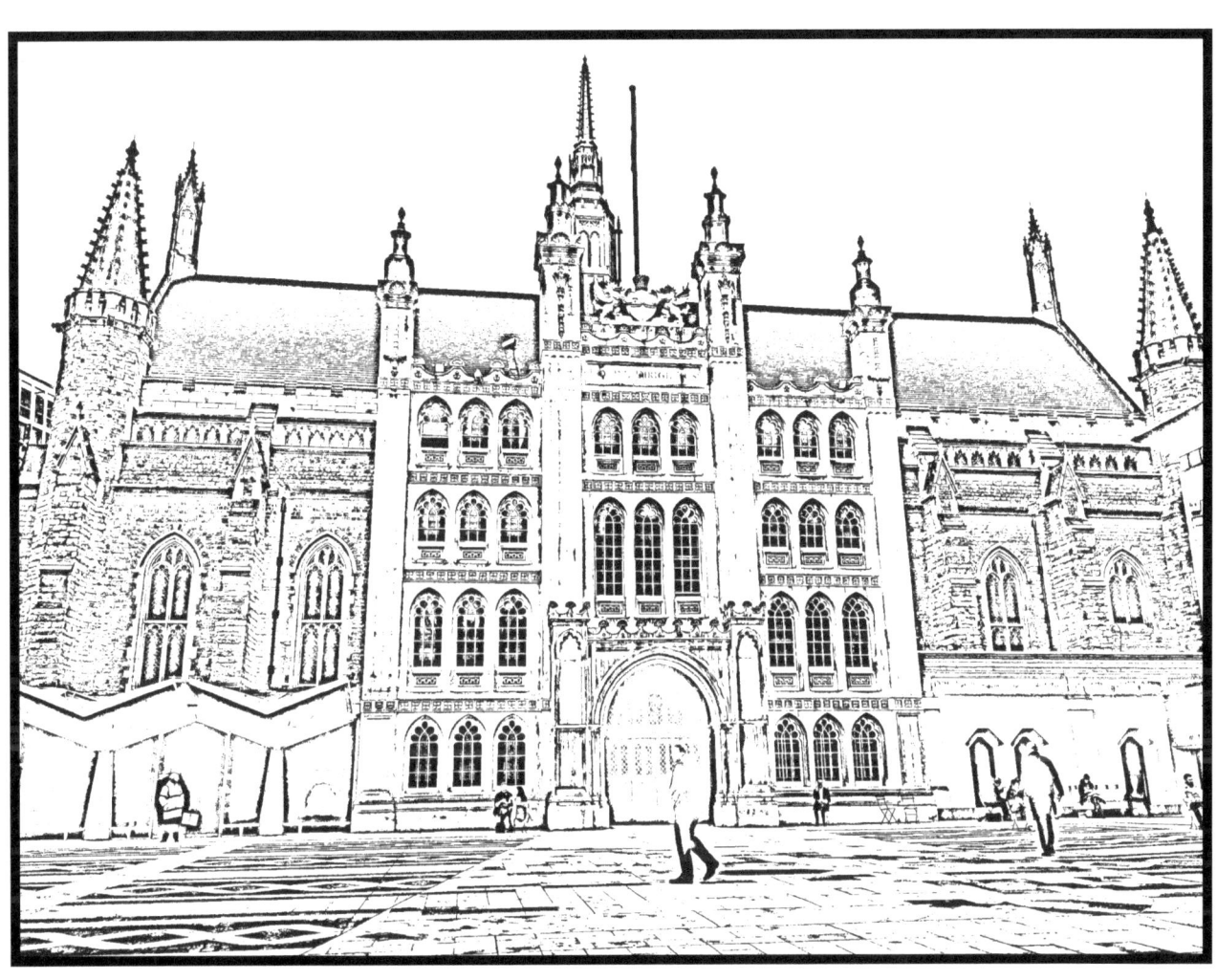

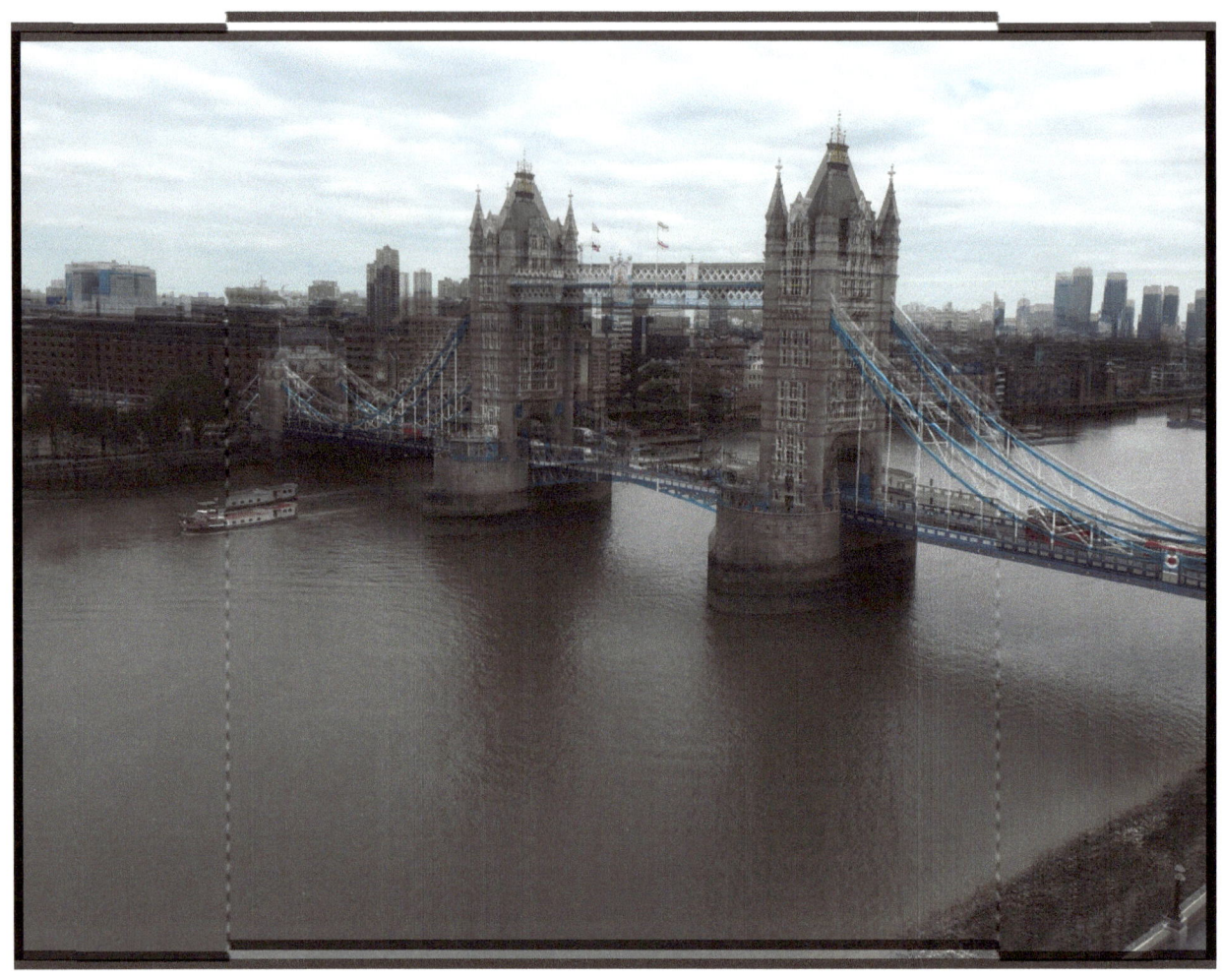

London SE1 2UP

The nearest tube stations to Tower Bridge is Tower Hill, London Bridge or Bermondsey. Tower Bridge crosses the River Thames close to The Tower of London. It was opened in 1894 by The Prince of Wales who became King Edward VII. A hydraulic system raises the Bridge to allow marine vessels to pass through. An exhibition is housed within the towers, high level walkway and Victorian engine rooms. Enjoy colouring.

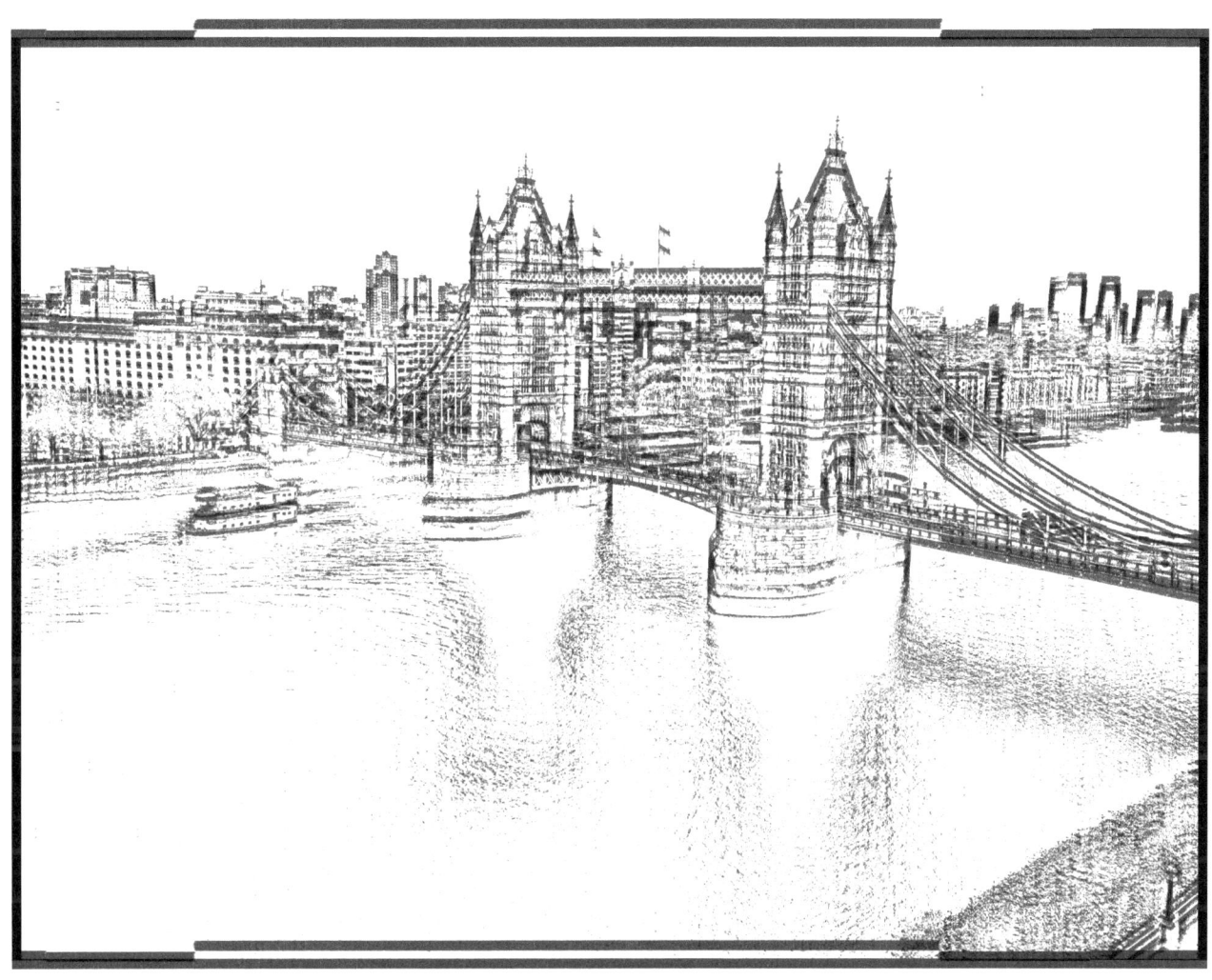

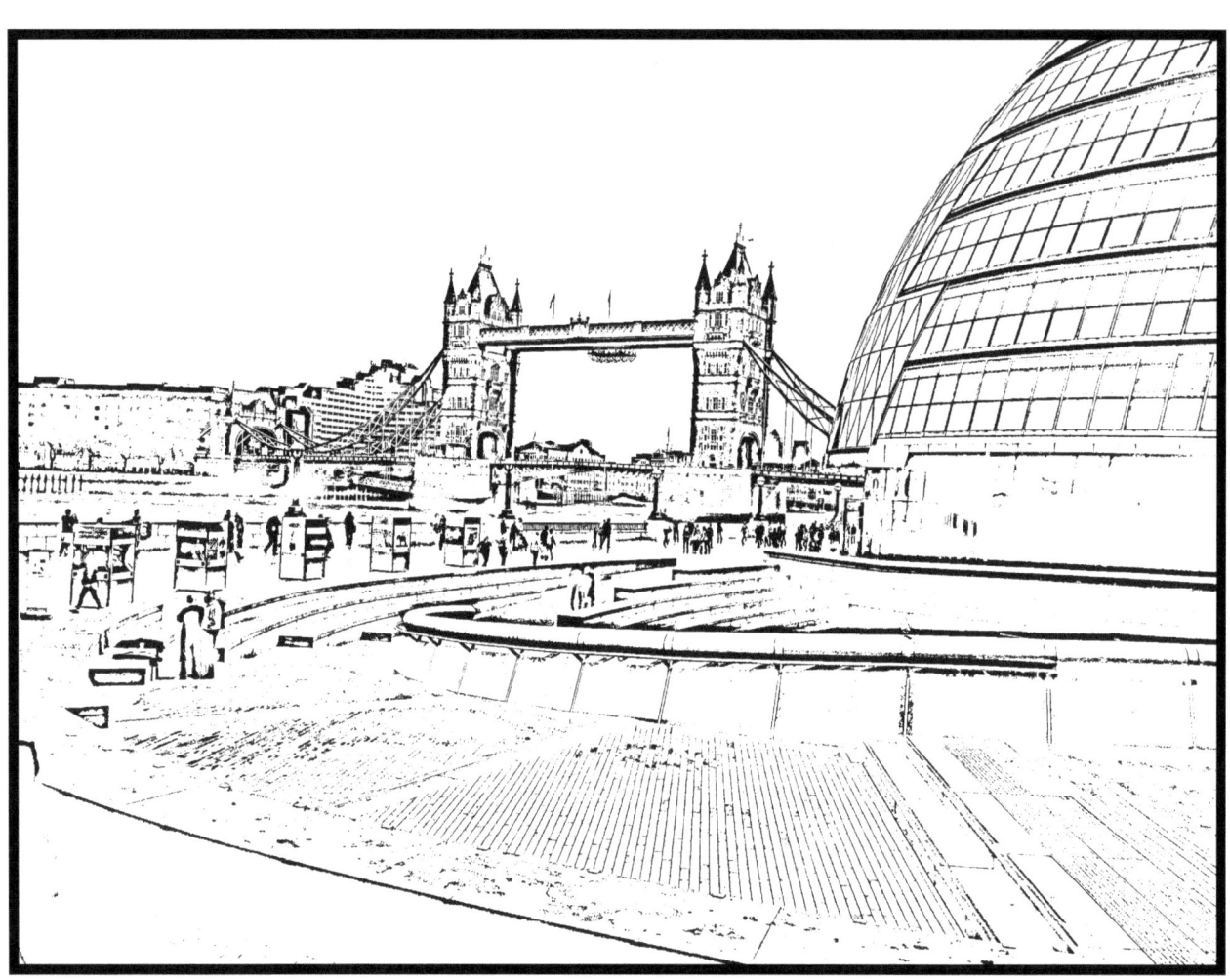

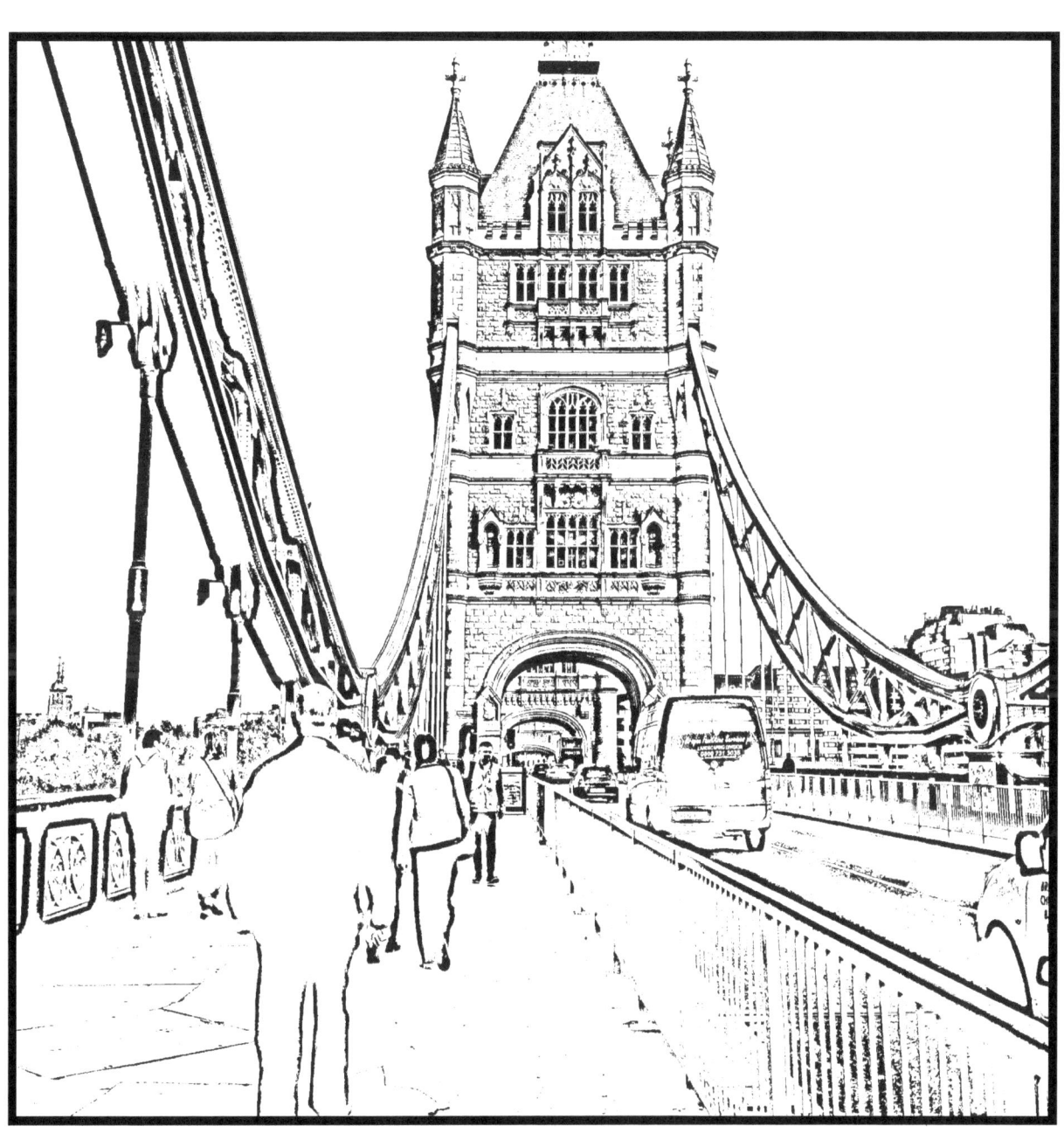

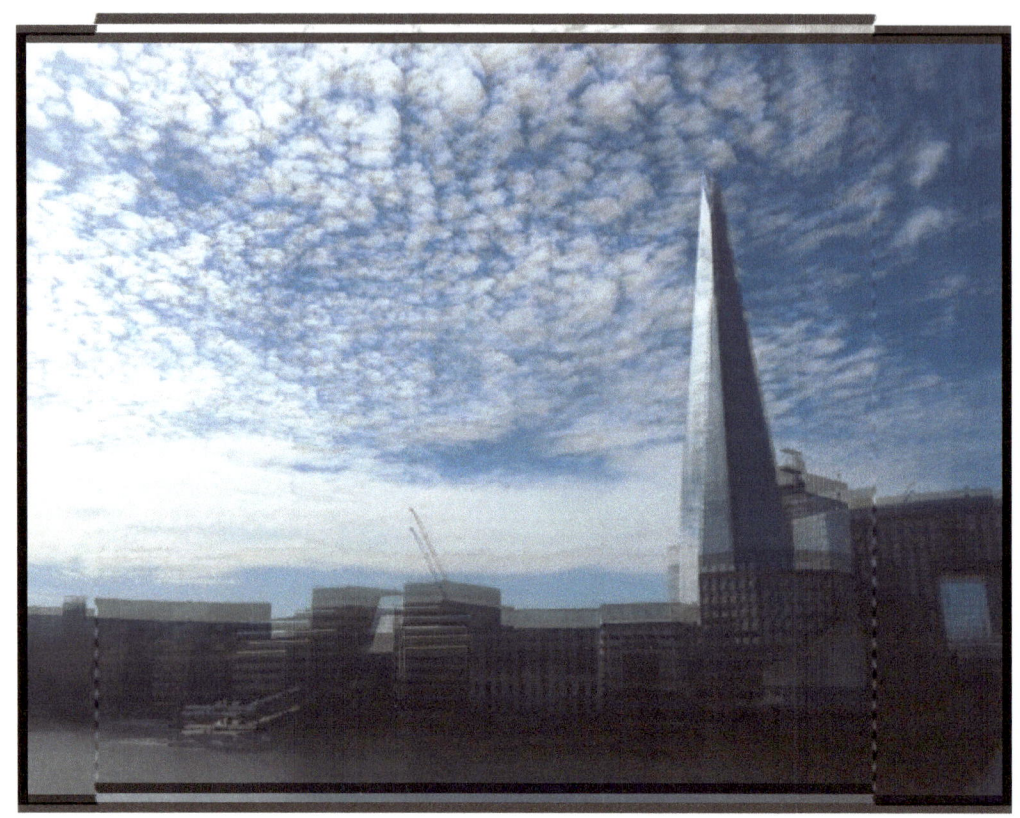

London SE1 9SG

The Shard, or Shard of Glass is the tallest building in the United Kingdom. It stands at 309.7 metres tall. Amazing views across London can be seen from the open air sky deck at the top. It is located just a few minutes from London Bridge tube station. The Shard was designed by Renzo Piano. Construction began in 2009 and it was opened in 2012. Enjoy colouring.

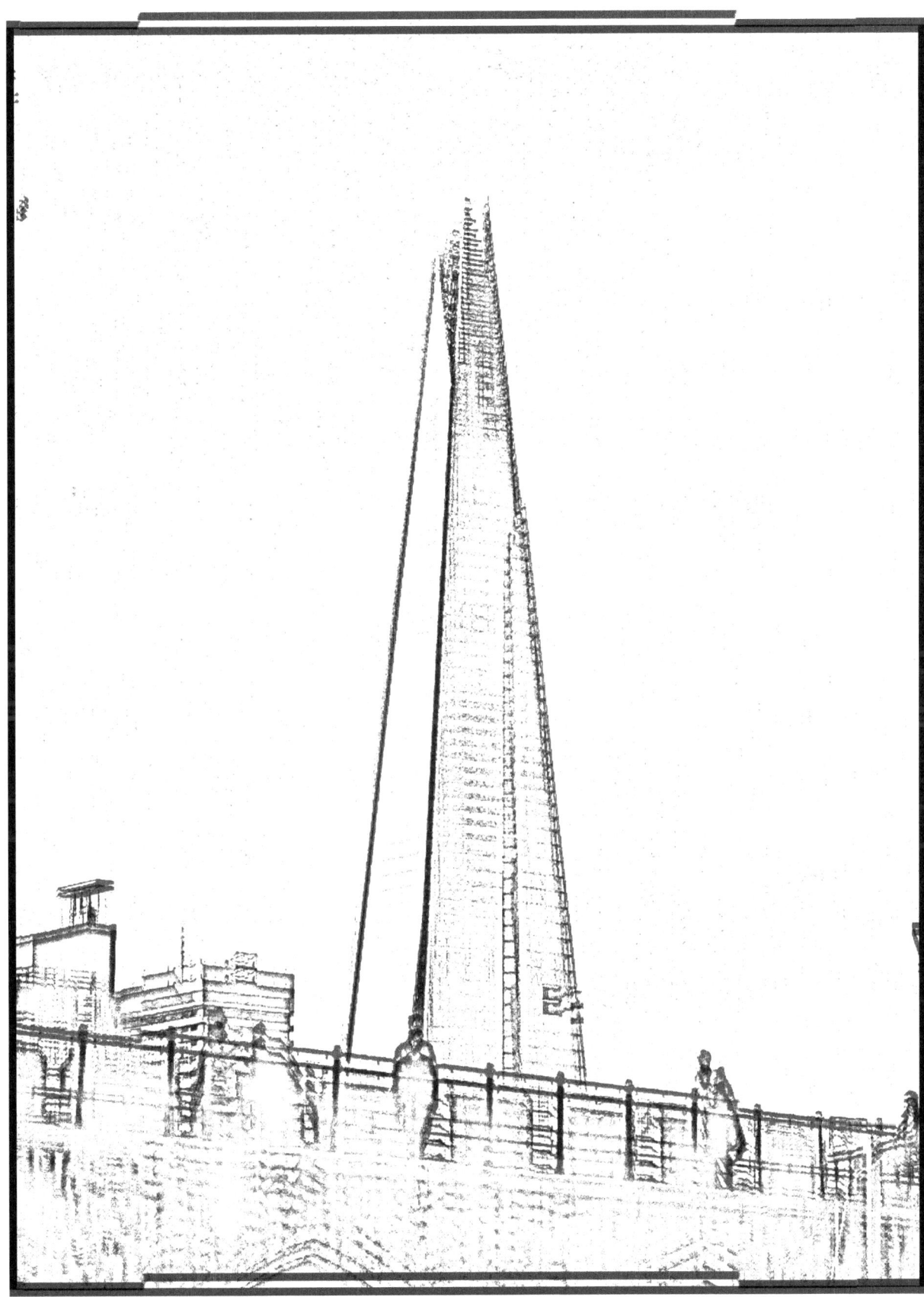

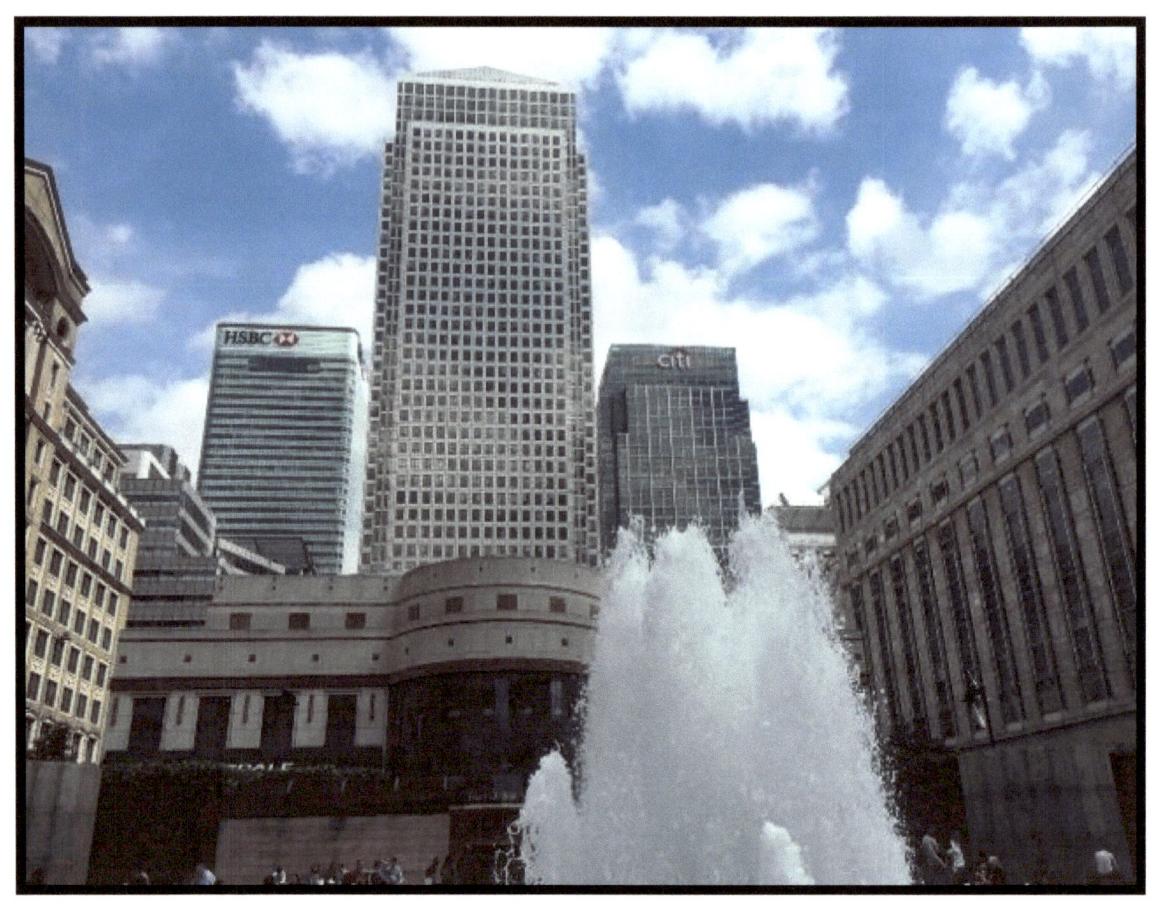

London E14 5AB

Canary Wharf is the second business district of London and is in the East of London within the borough of Tower Hamlets. It is a major financial centre and houses One Canada Square, the second tallest building in the United Kingdom. Over 100,000 people work in Canary Wharf in many major banks such as JP Morgan, Credit Suisse, Citigroup, HSBC and Barclays to name a few. It is located on the West India Docks. The nearest tube station is Canary Wharf. Enjoy colouring.

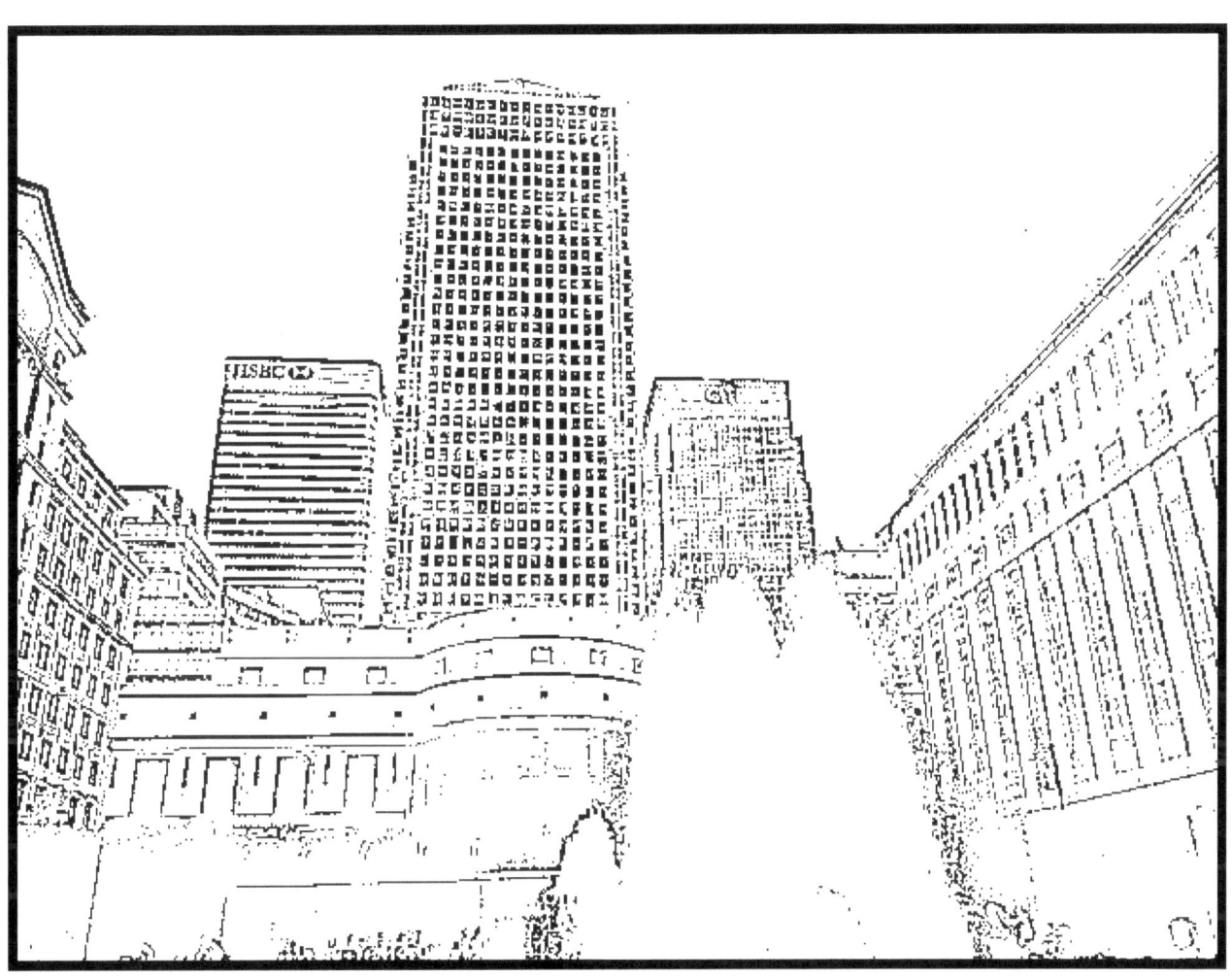

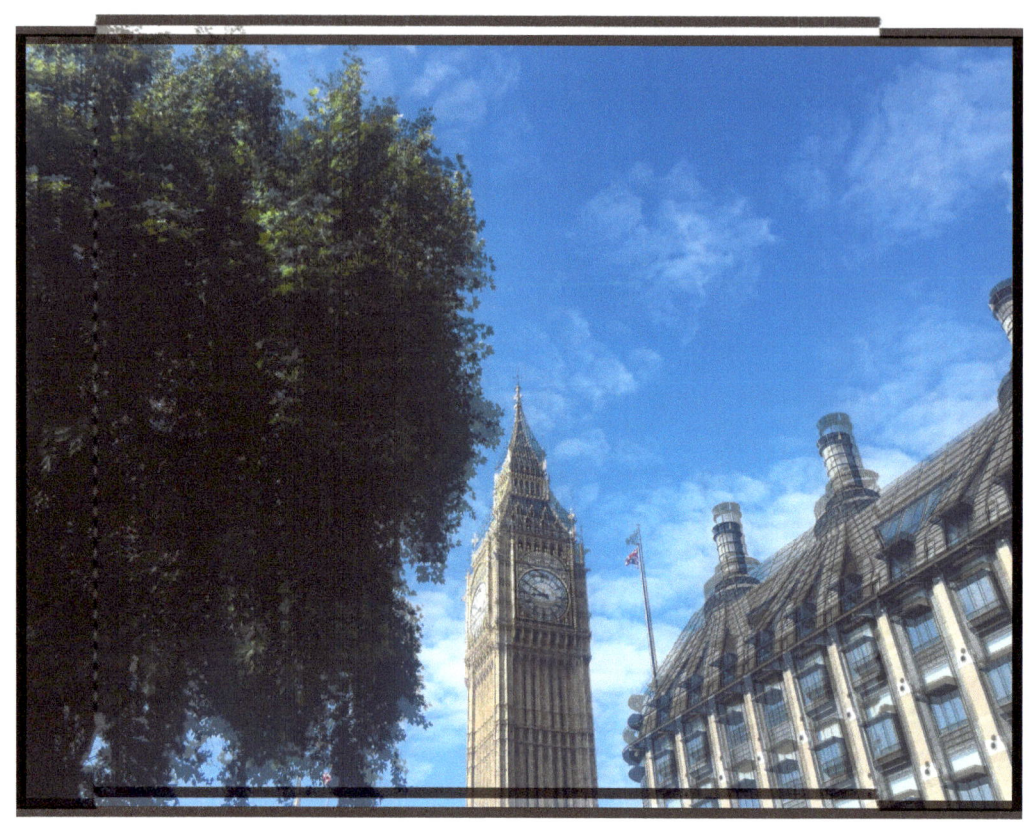

London SW1A 0AA

The Palace of Westminster is where the two Houses of the United Kingdom Parliament meet. One is The House of Commons and the other is The House of Lords. It remains a royal palace and is also the seat of the Royal Courts of Justice which meet in Westminster Hall. The Elizabeth Tower houses the bell "Big Ben" which is a famous tourist attraction. The palace is close to Westminster Abbey from which it derives is name. Nearest tube stations are Westminster and St. James' Park Enjoy colouring.

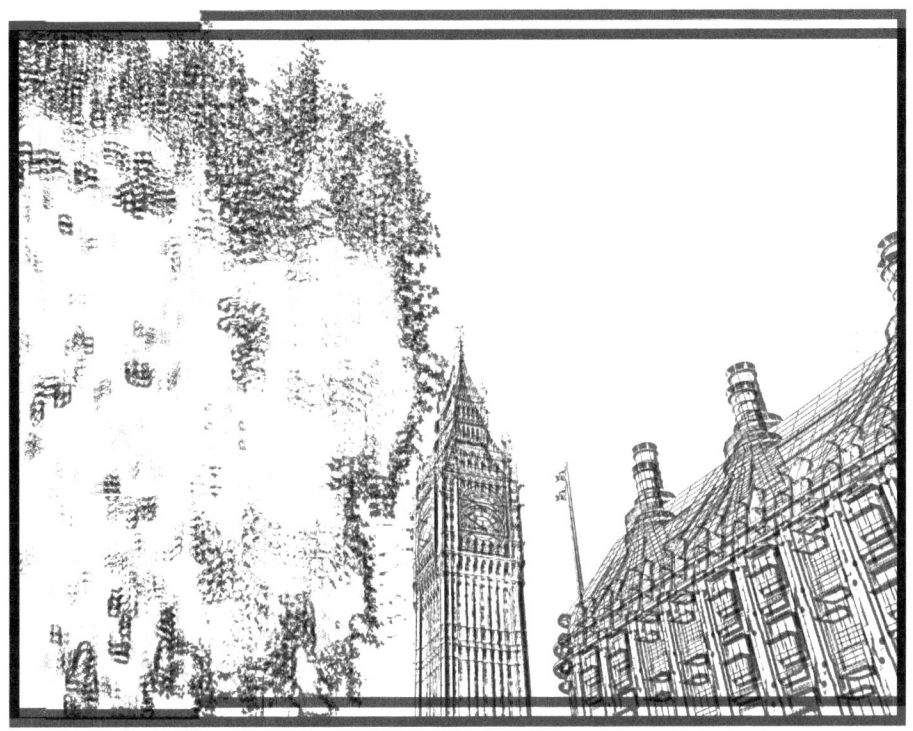

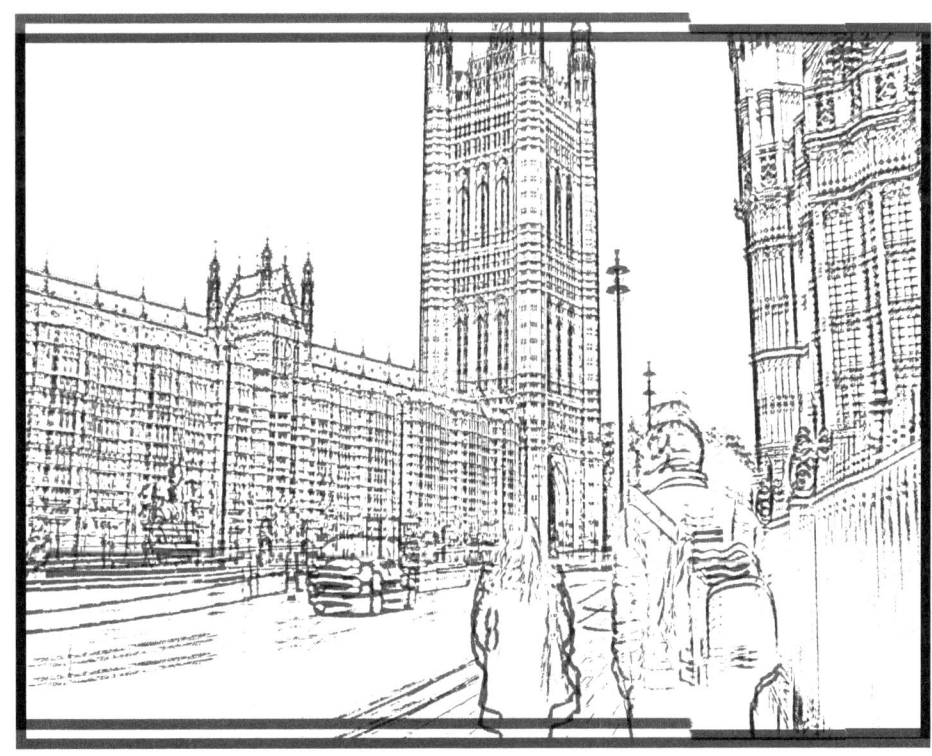

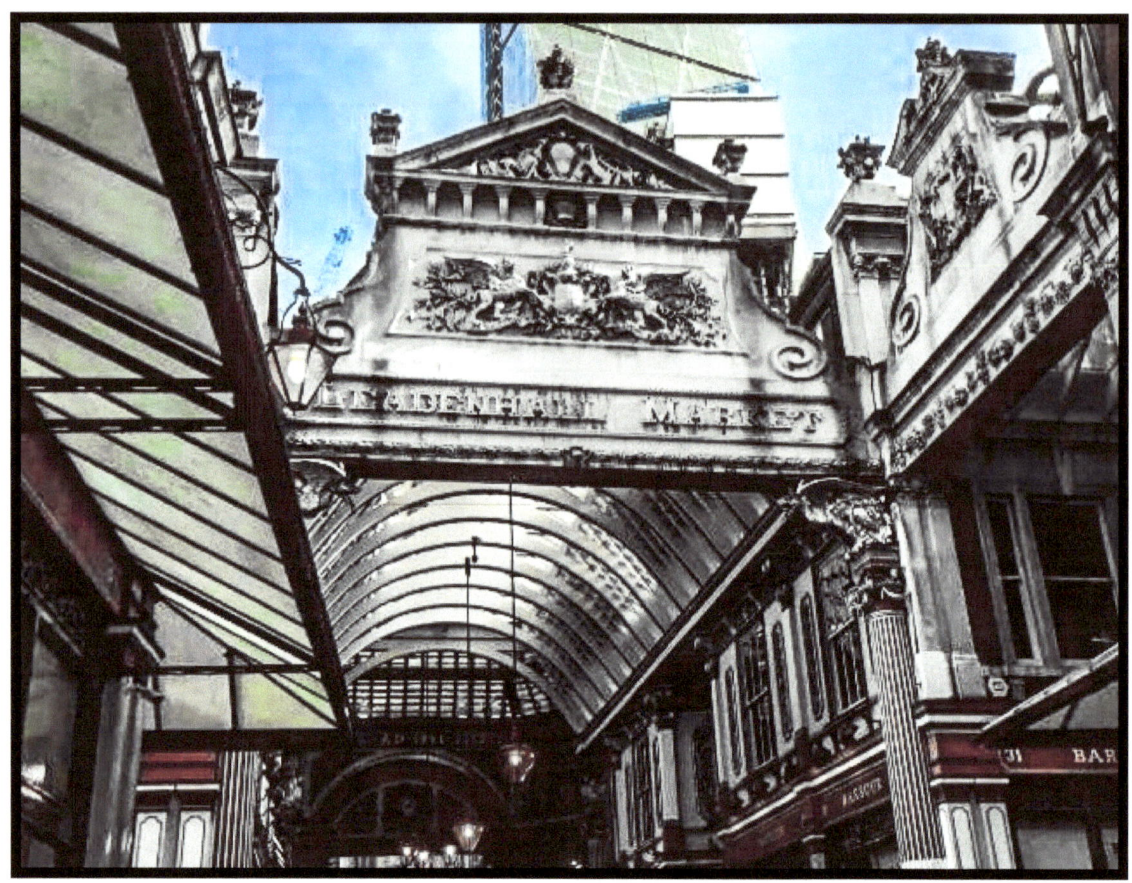

London EC3V 1LT

London has many markets, such as Borough market, Smithfields, Petticoat Lane and Leadenhall market. Leadenhall market is one of London's oldest, dating back to the 14th century and is sited in the centre of the City of London. It sells fresh foods. Butchers and fishmongers can be found here. Its architecture makes it a favourite tourist attraction and it was filmed during the making of "Harry Potter and the Philosopher's Stone".

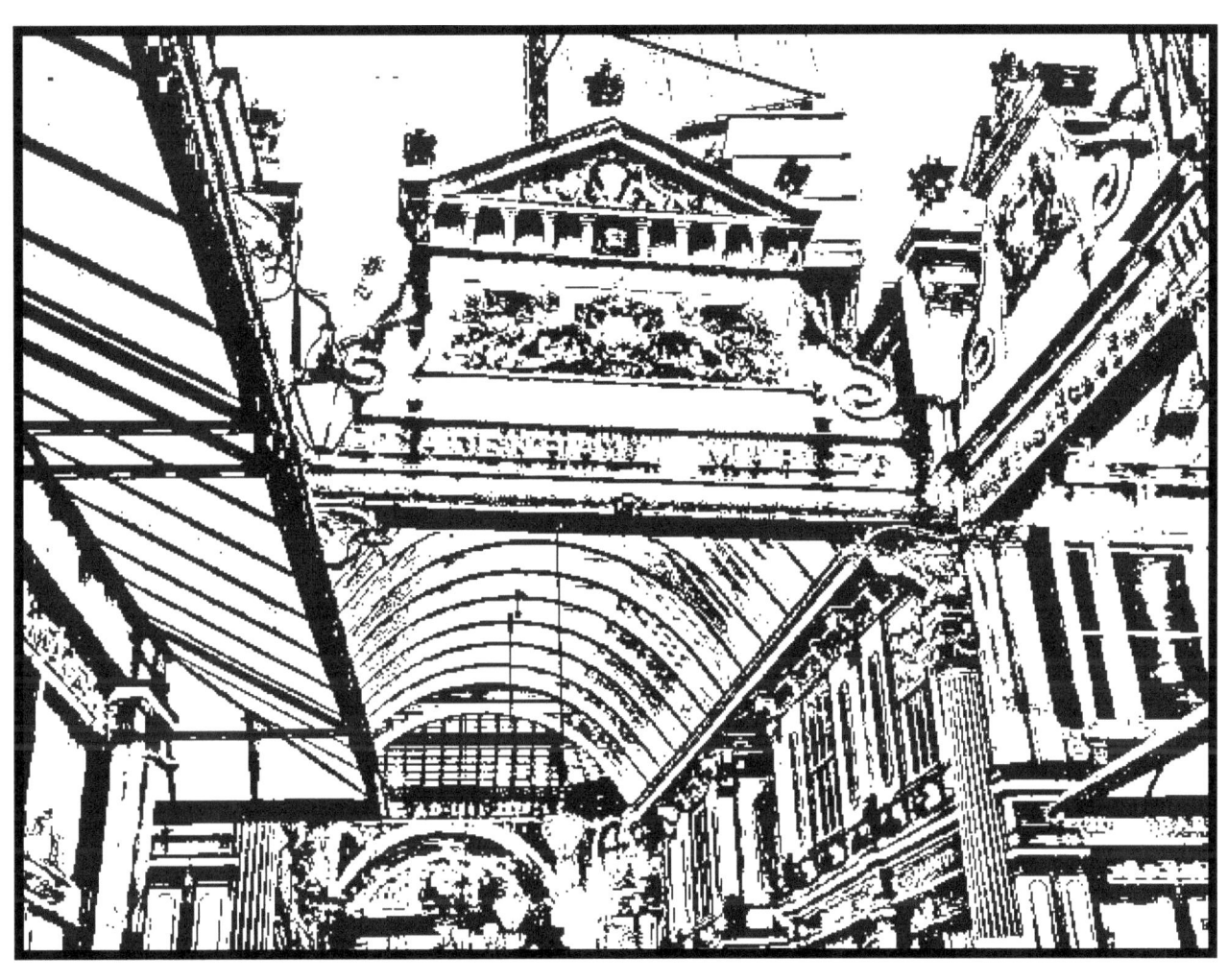

There is in London all that life can afford.

Samuel Johnson.

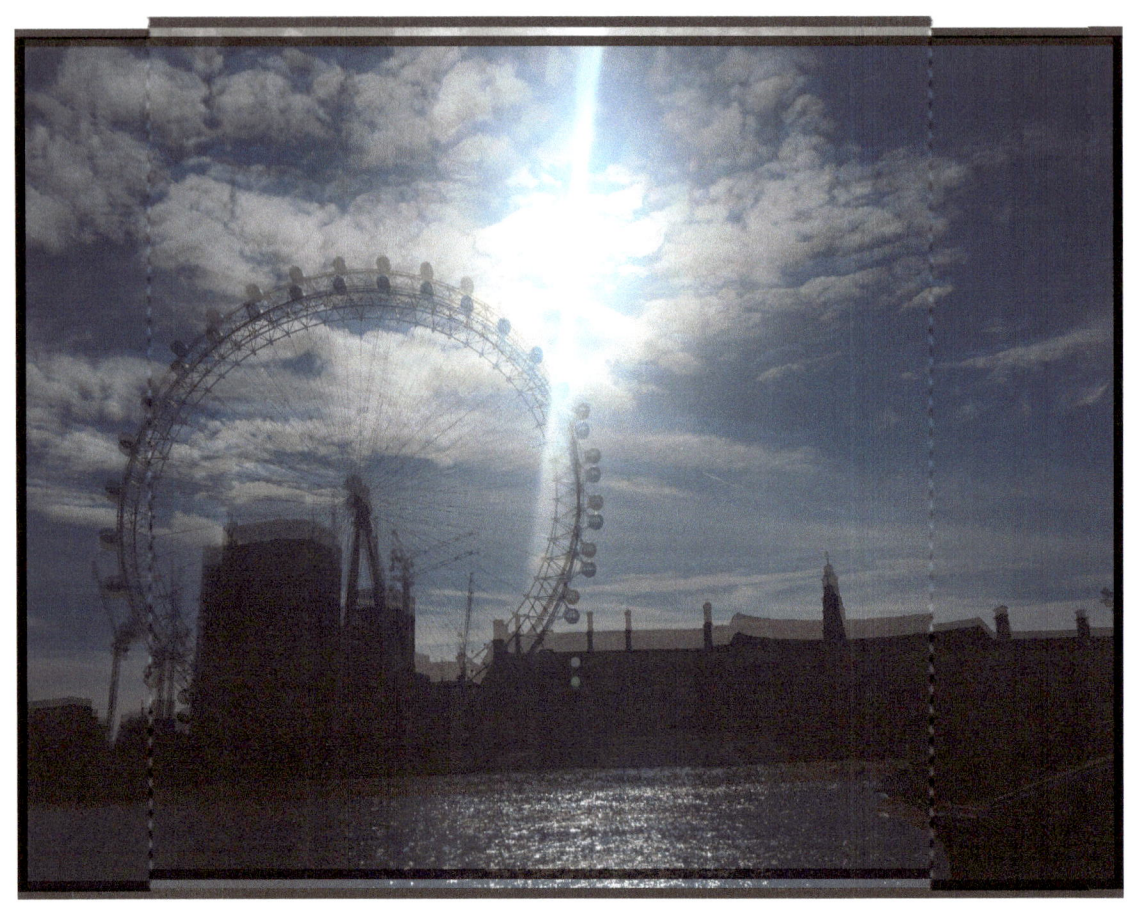

London SE1 7PB

The London Eye is sited on the South bank of the River Thames. It is a large ferris wheel with thirty two carriages. It opened officially in 1999 and began to take passengers in March 2000. It takes about 30 minutes to complete one full revolution and its speed is slow enough that it does not need to stop when people embark or disembark. Nearest tube station is Waterloo. Enjoy colouring.

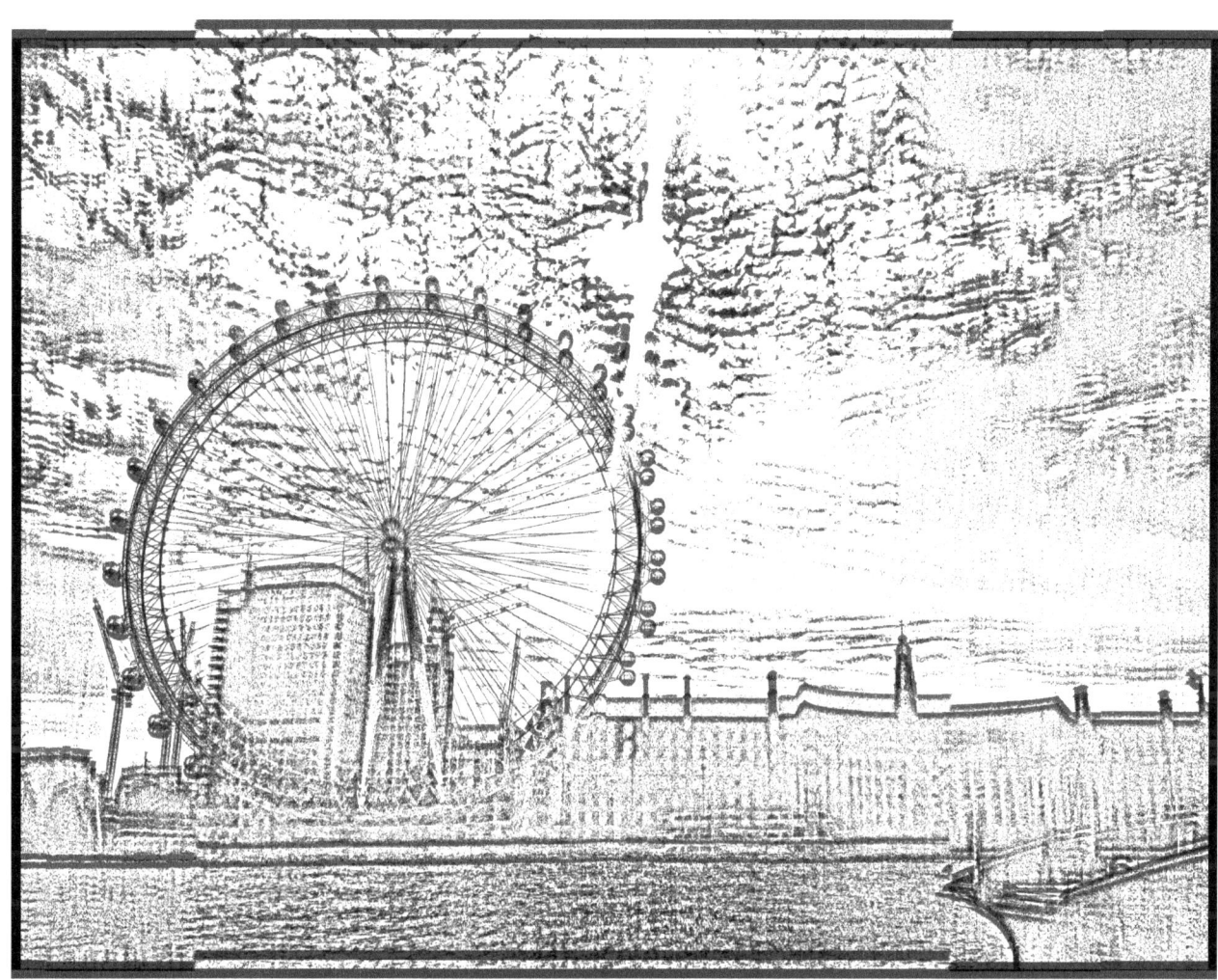

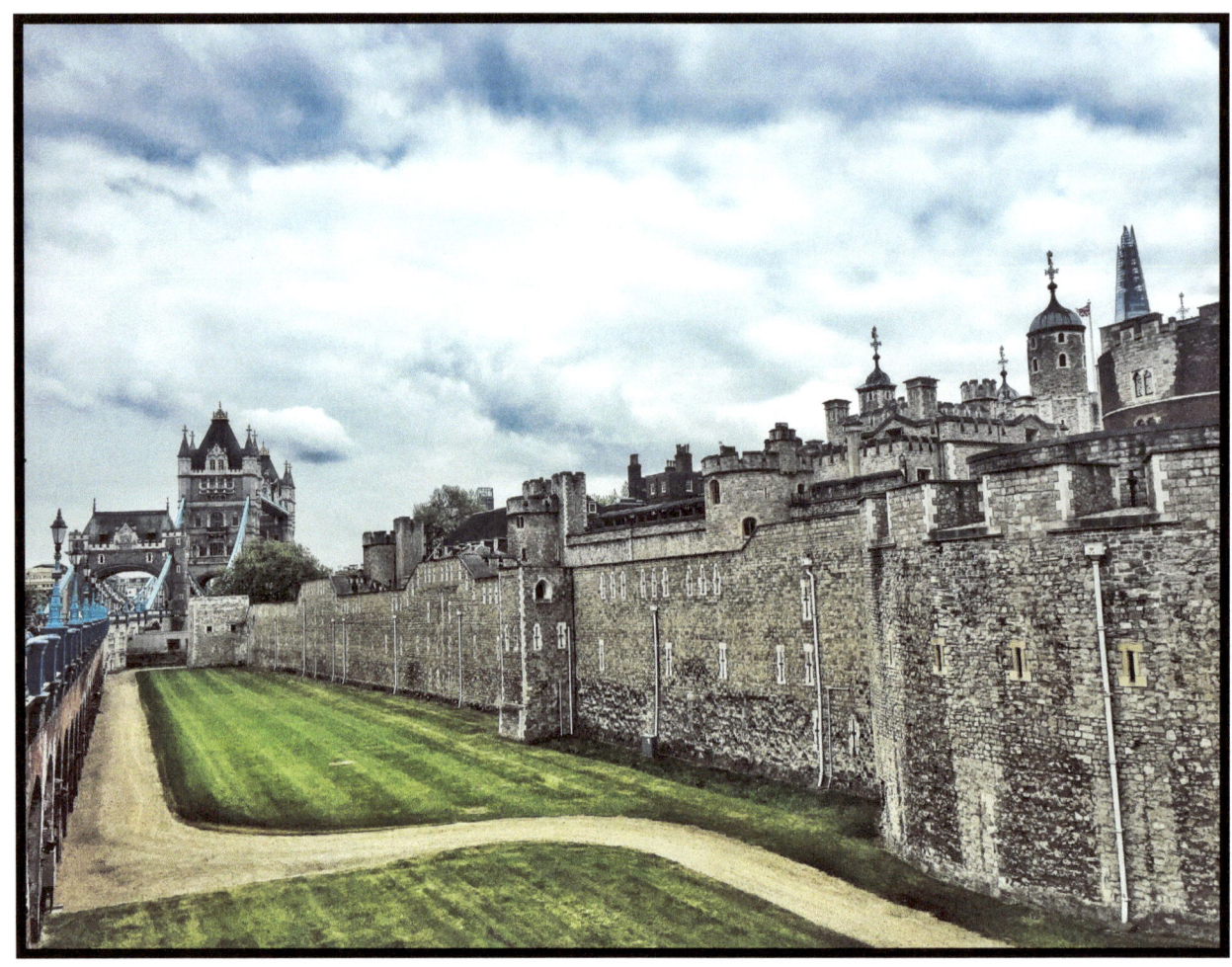

London EC3N 4AB

The Tower of London dates back to around 1066 during the Norman Conquest. It has been a prison and an armoury. It has housed the Royal Mint and is still the home of The Crown Jewels.Many ghosts are said to walk the grounds of the Tower, including Ann Boleyn, Lady Jane Grey, Henry VI and the Princes in the Tower.Famous prisoners include the Kray twins, Rudolf Hess, Guy Fawkes, Thomas Cromwell and Sir Walter Raleigh. Nearest tube station is Tower Hill. Enjoy colouring.

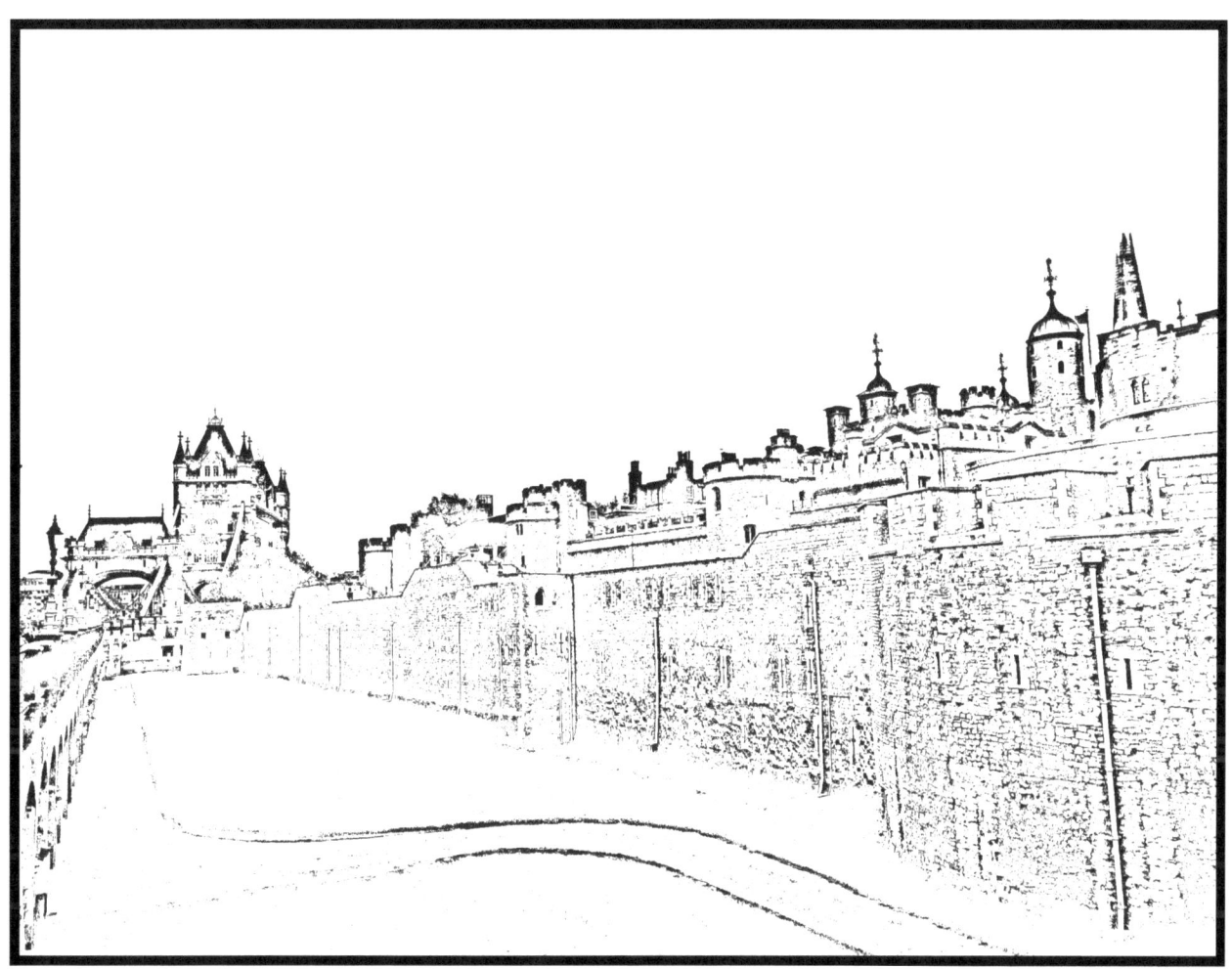

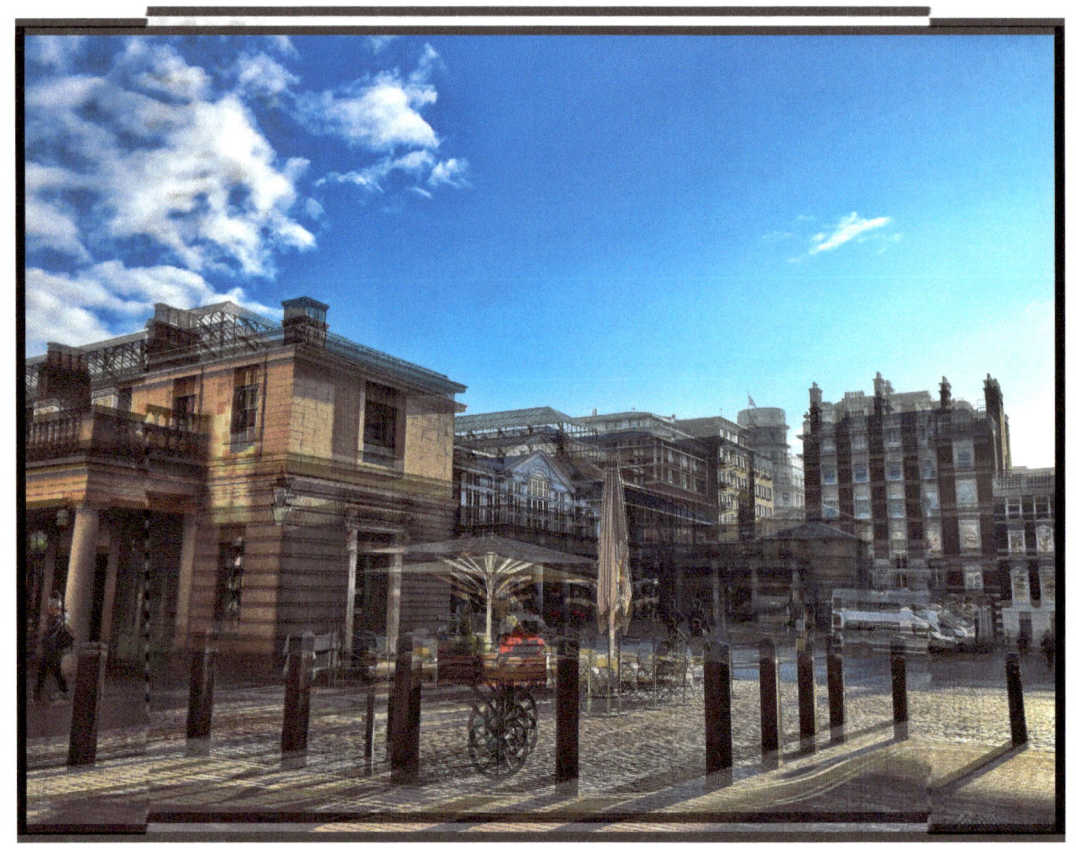

London WC2E 9DB

Covent Garden was previously well known as a fruit and vegetable market. Now, it is a shopping centre and tourist area, with the Royal Opera House, known simply as "Covent Garden". In 1200 it produced fruit and vegetables for Westminster Abbey. The land was given to the Earl of Bedford by Henry VIII. He commissioned housing for wealthy tenants. Nowadays it is a major tourist attraction with restaurants, shops, cafes and pubs. Nearest tube station is Covet Garden. Enjoy colouring.

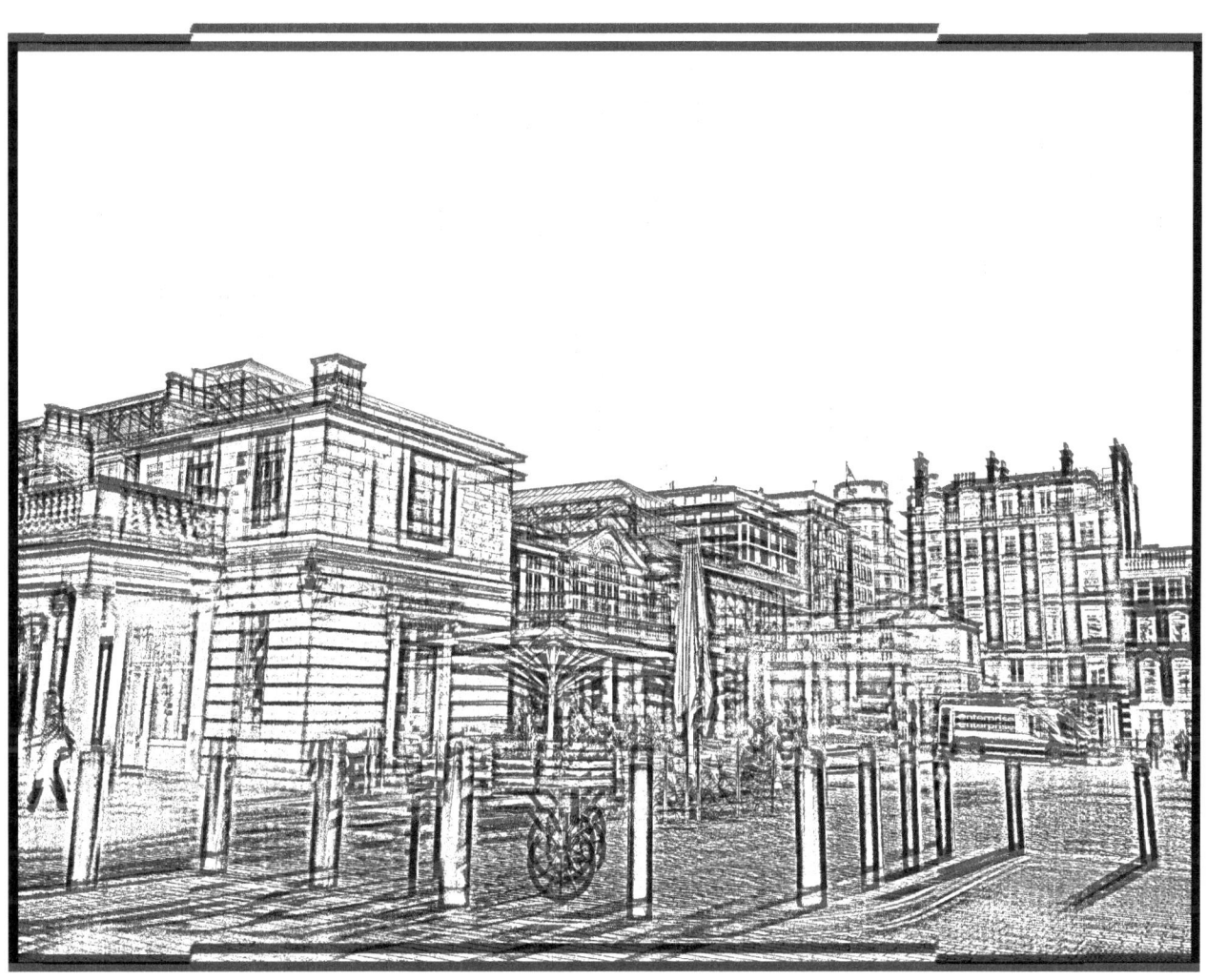

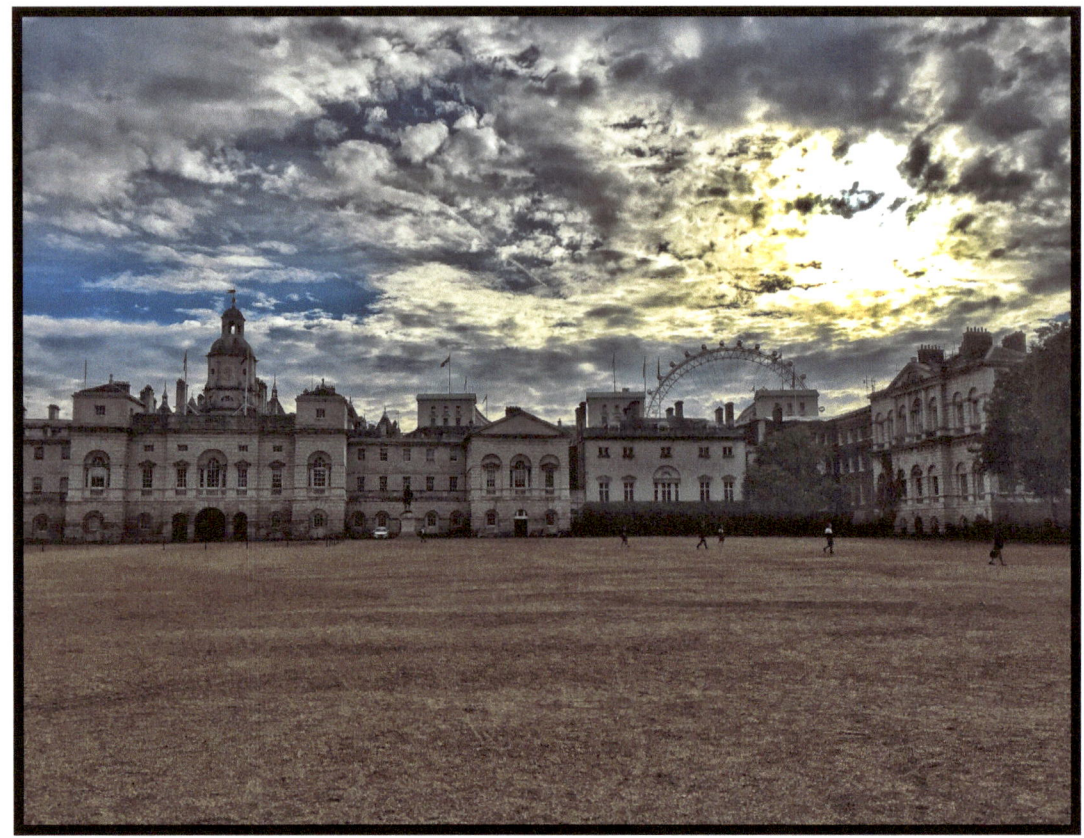

London SW1A 2AX

Horse Guards' Parade is a large parade ground where the monarch's official birthday is marked with The Trooping of the Colour and where the ceremony of Beating the Retreat is held. During Henry VIII's reign, tournaments, such as jousting, were held here. During the 2012 Olympic Games, the Olympic beach volleyball competition was held here. Nearest tube stations are Westminster and Charing Cross. Enjoy colouring.

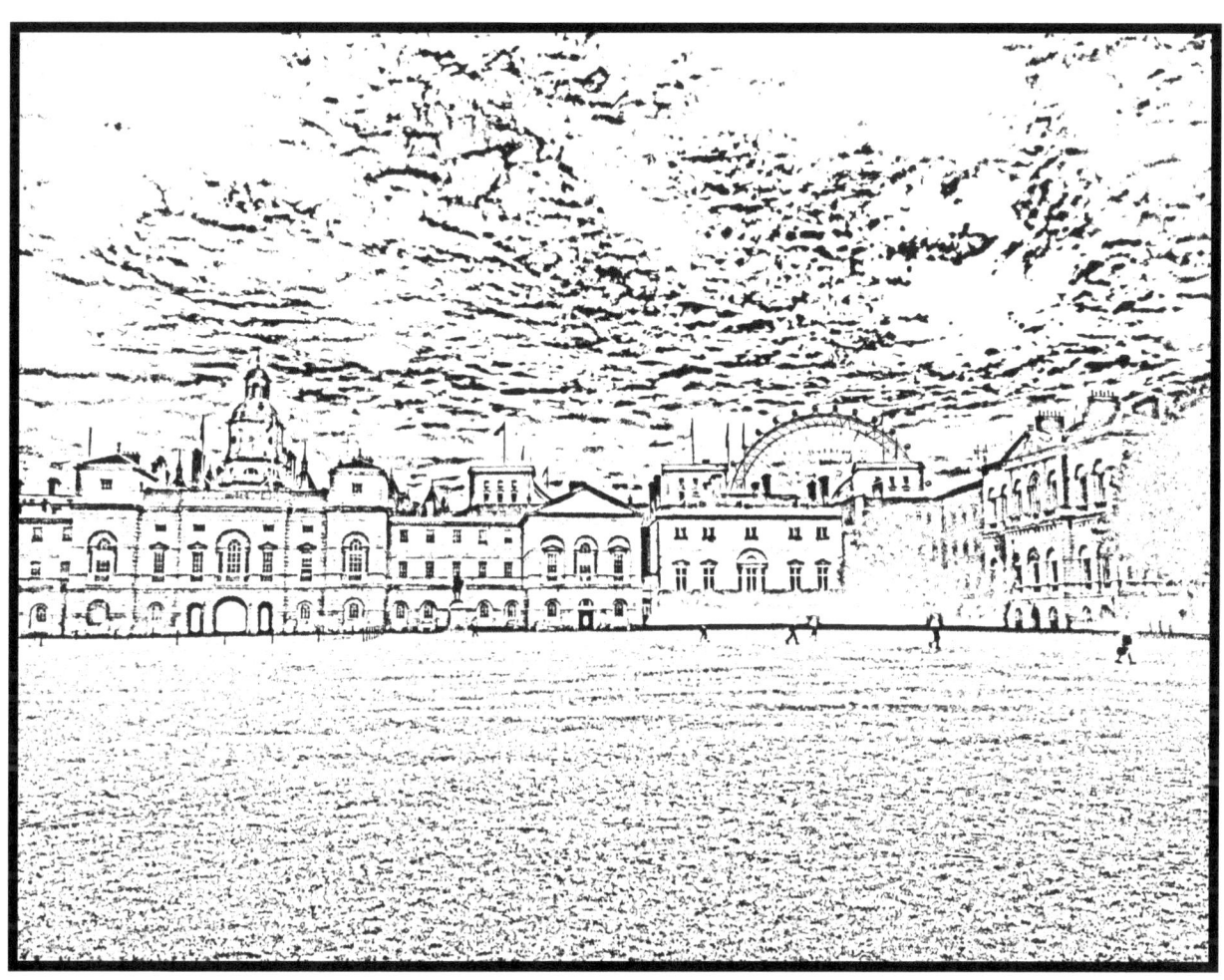

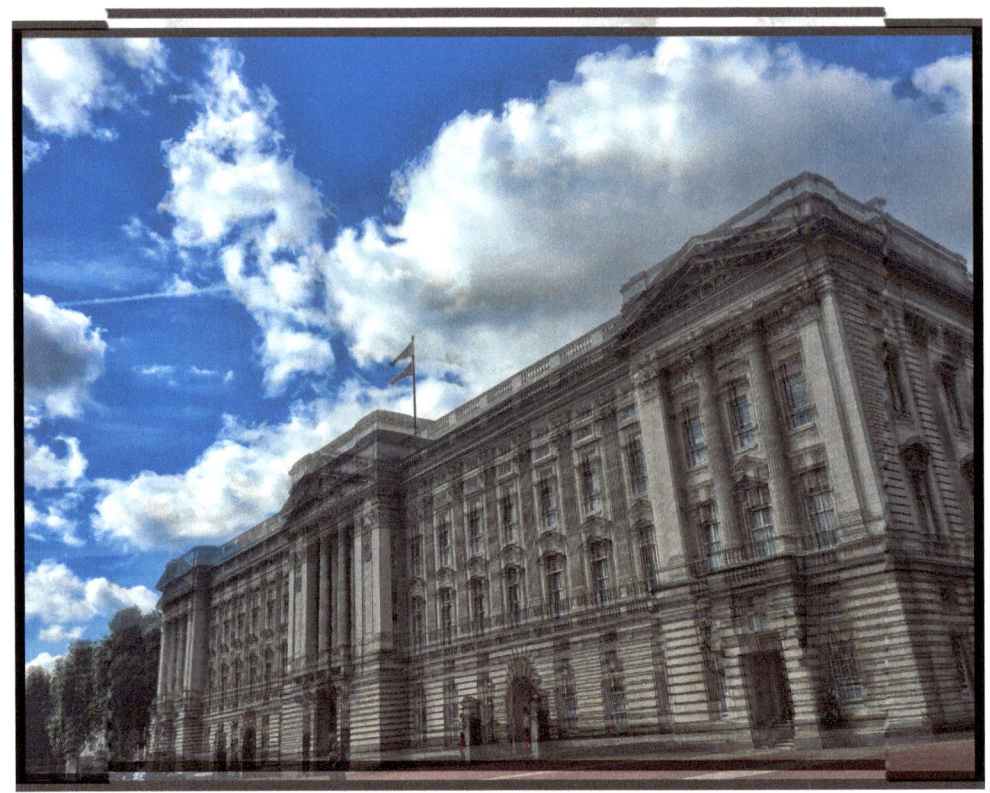

London SW1W 0BT

Buckingham Palace is the London residence of the reigning monarch. It was acquired by King George III for his wife. Queen Victoria moved in after renovation and enlargement in 1837. The Royal Family greets the people from the famous balcony in the East Front. Investitures, state banquets and other ceremonies are held here. Nearest tube station is Victoria. Enjoy colouring.

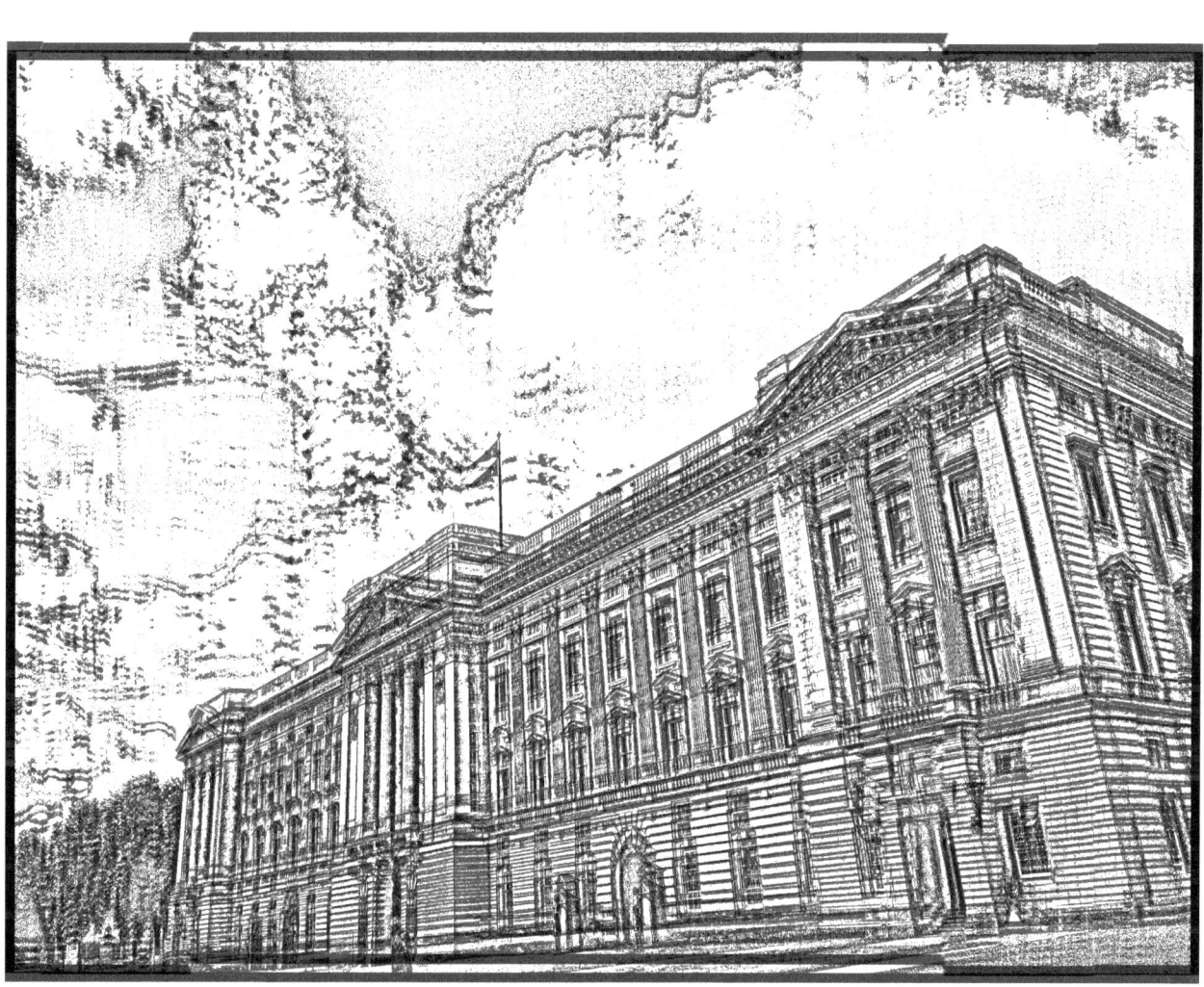

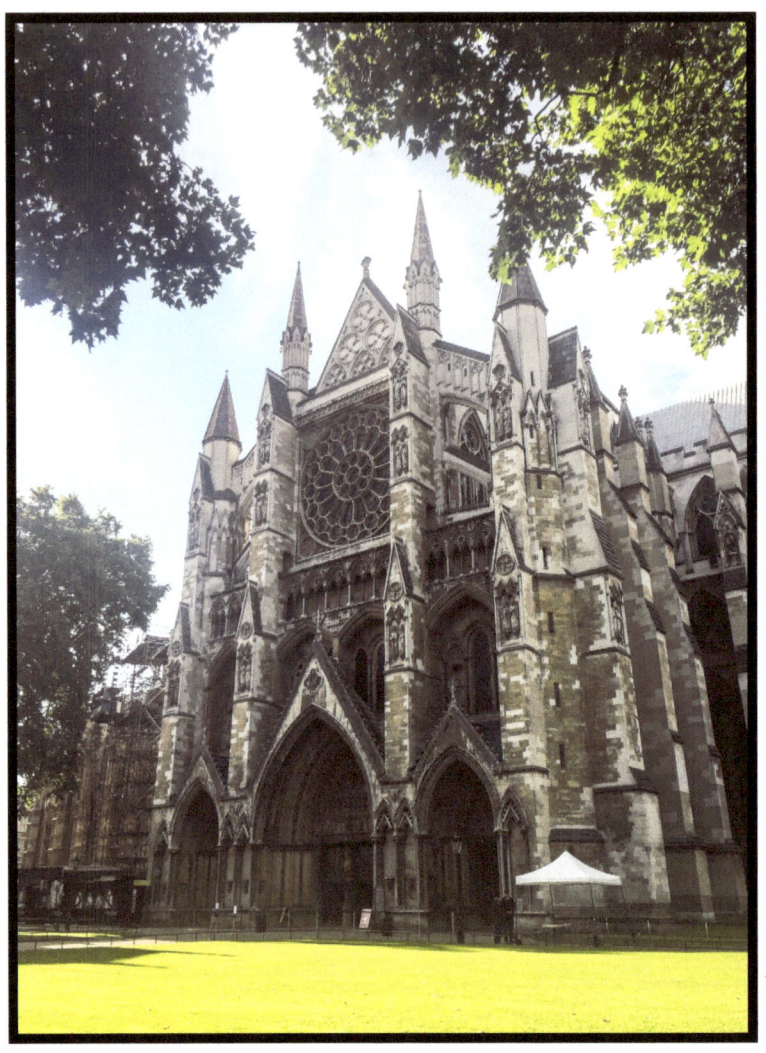

London SW1P 3PA

Westminster Abbey is one of the United Kingdom's most famous religious buildings. It is the traditional place for British monarchs to be crowned and to be buried. Many royal weddings have been held in the Abbey too. In the Abbey floor is the tomb of The Unknown Warrior. It is the only tomb on which it is forbidden to walk. Nearest tube station is Westminster. Enjoy colouring.

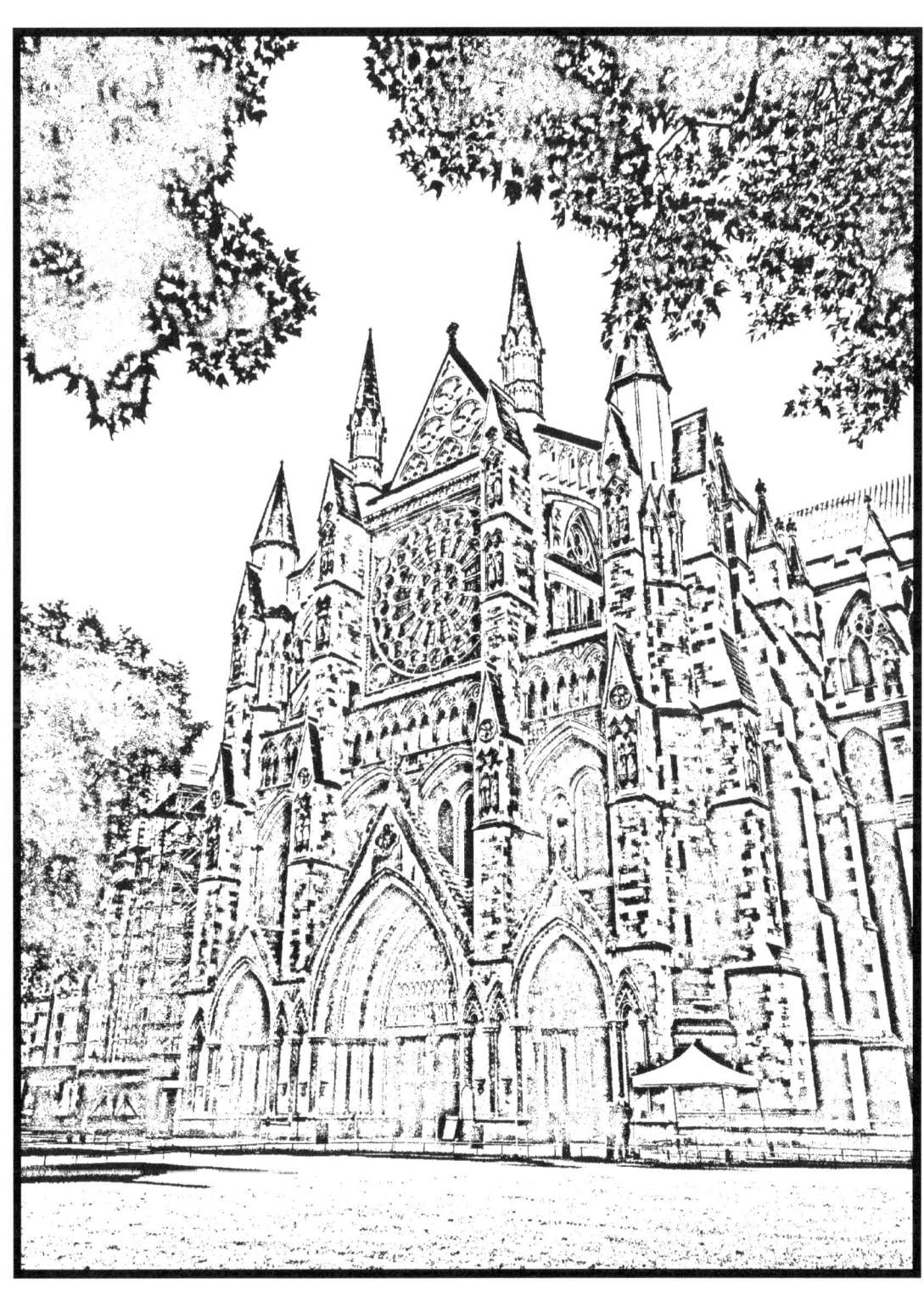

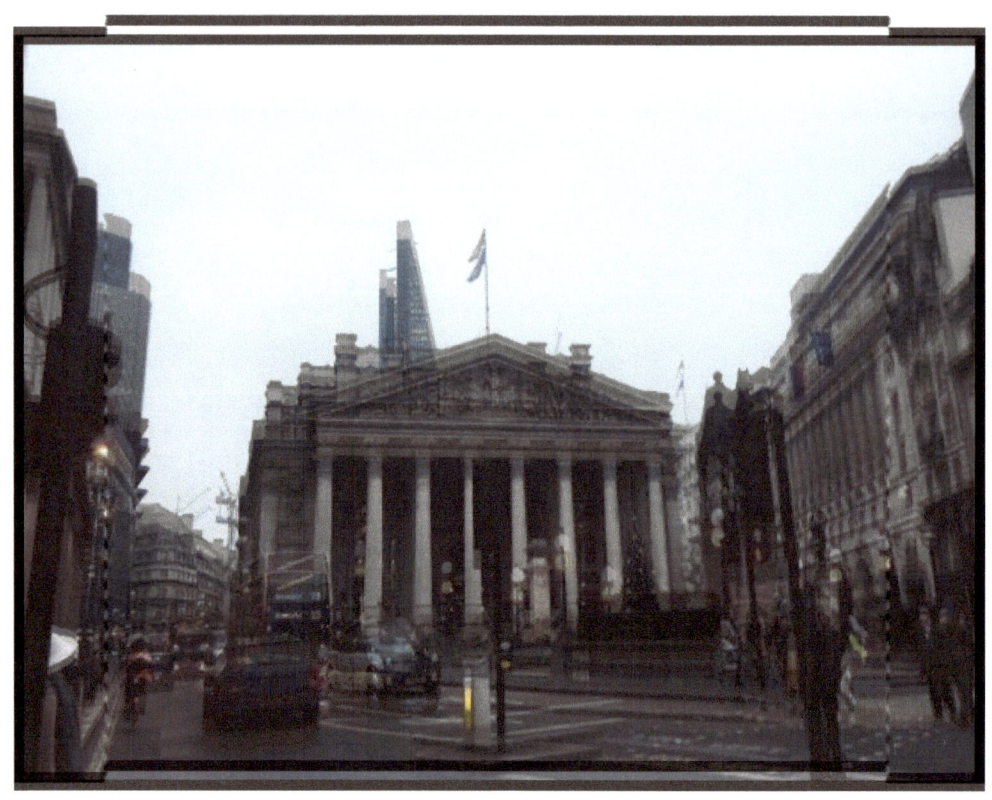

London EC3V 3LR

The Royal Exchange opened in 1571, over 400 years ago, to be the commercial centre of the City of London. It is to be found between Threadneedle Street and Cornhill. From the steps of the Royal Exchange, a crier or herald would proclaim a new monarch's reign to the public. It consists of four sides surrounding a central courtyard within which merchants and tradesmen could do their business. Nowadays, boutiques and restaurants have joined the retailers. The nearest tube stations are Bank, Monument and Cannon Street. Enjoy colouring.

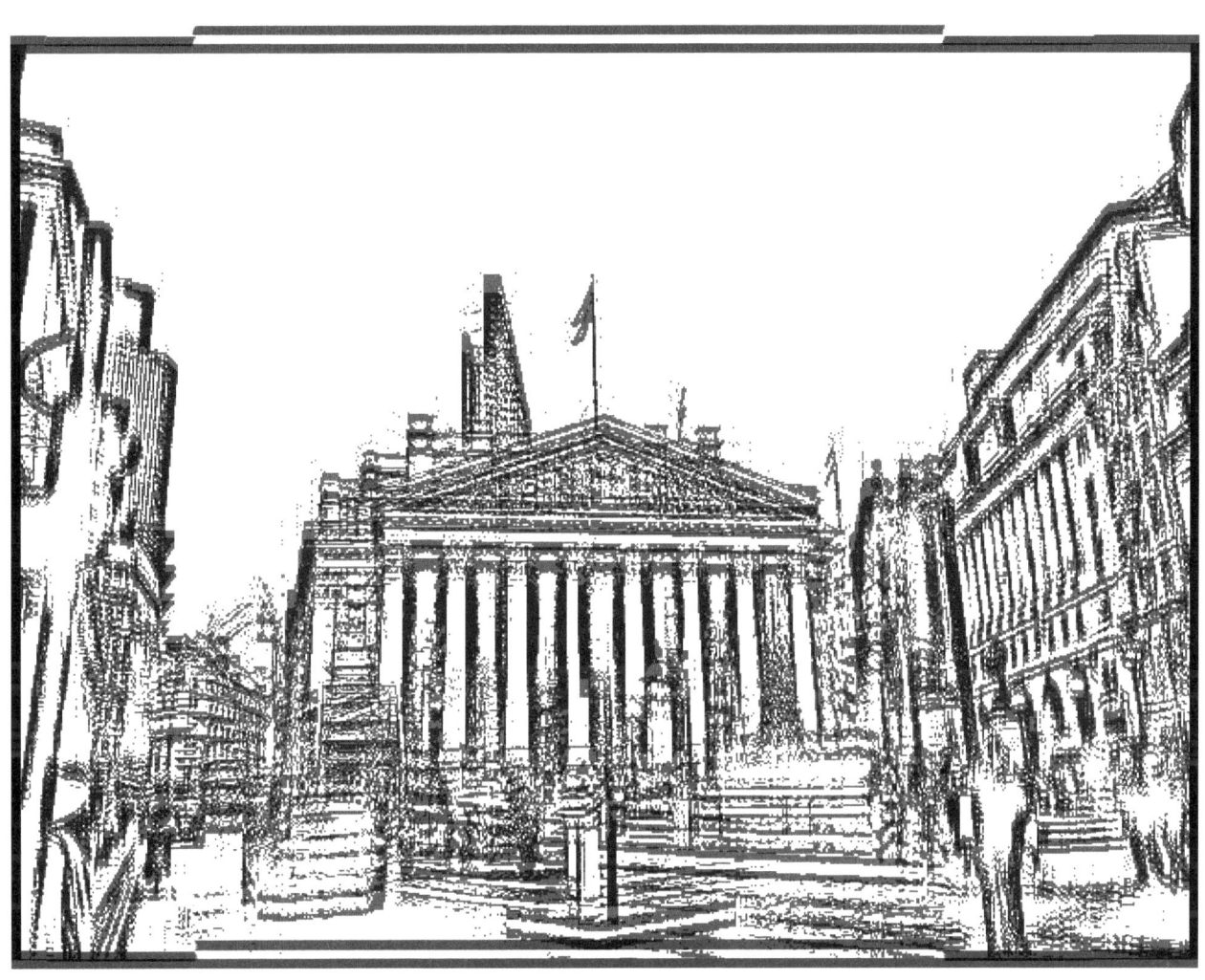

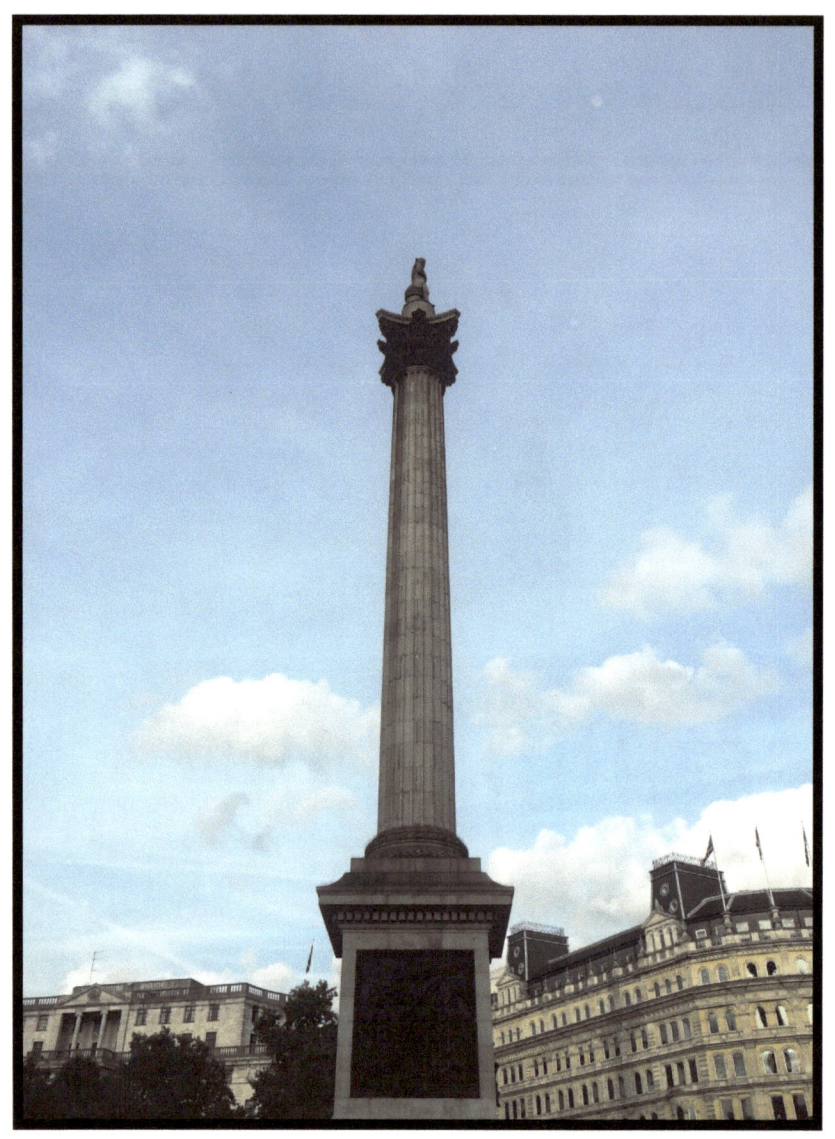

London WC2N 5DX

Trafalgar Square is a public square whose name commemorates The Battle of Trafalgar fought during The Napoleonic Wars. It is often used for public and political demonstrations. Every Christmas, a Christmas tree donated by Norway is erected for 12 days before and after Christmas Day. In the centre is Nelson's Column; to the north is the National gallery, to the east is St. Martin's- in- the-Fields, to the south is Whitehall and to the south west is The Mall, via Admiralty Arch, which leads to Buckingham Palace. Nearest tube station is Charing Cross. Enjoy colouring.

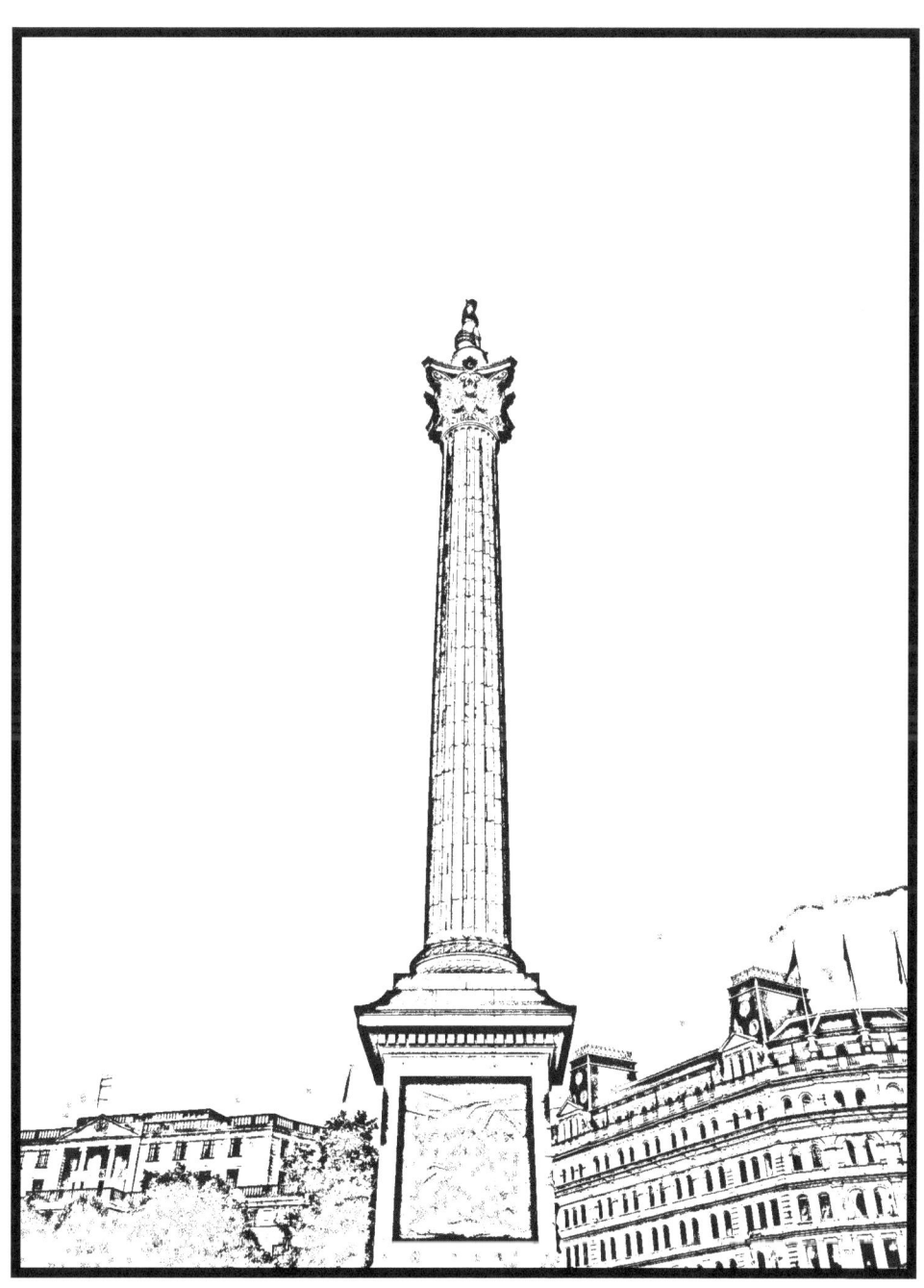

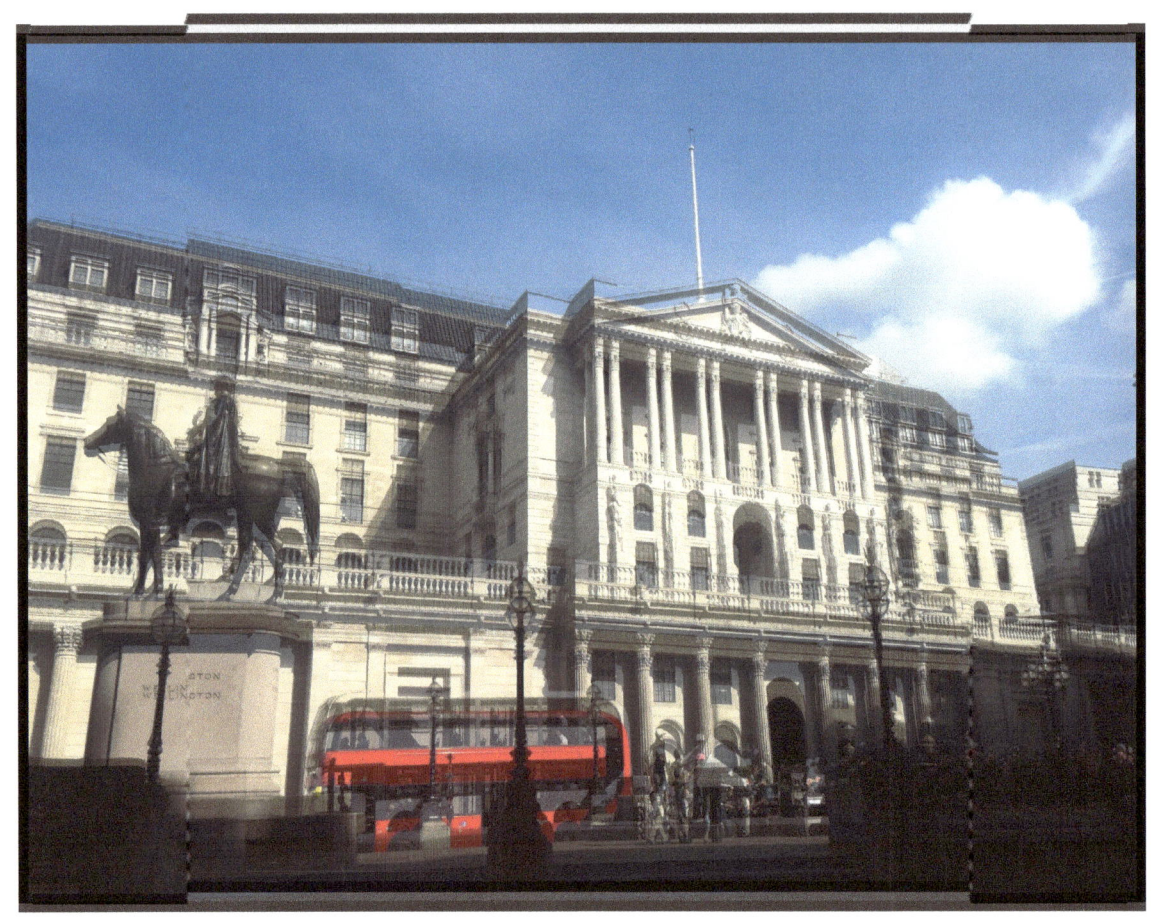

London EC2R 8AH

The Bank of England is the Central Bank of the United Kingdom. Its headquarters have been on Threadneedle Street near The Royal Exchange since 1734 and is therefore fondly called "The Old Lady of Threadneedle Street". It is custodian to the official gold reserves of the United Kingdom. Nearest tube station is Bank. Enjoy colouring.

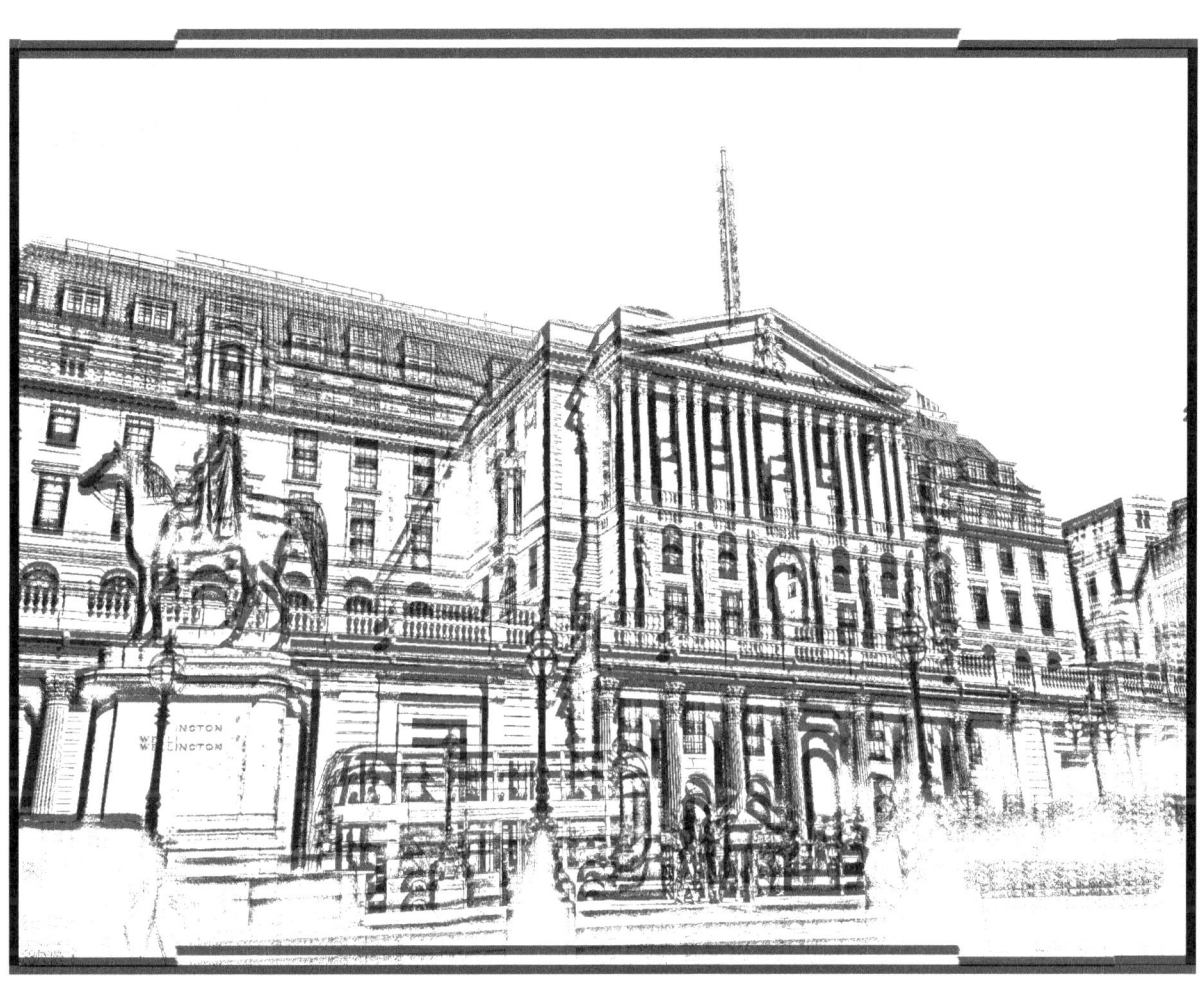

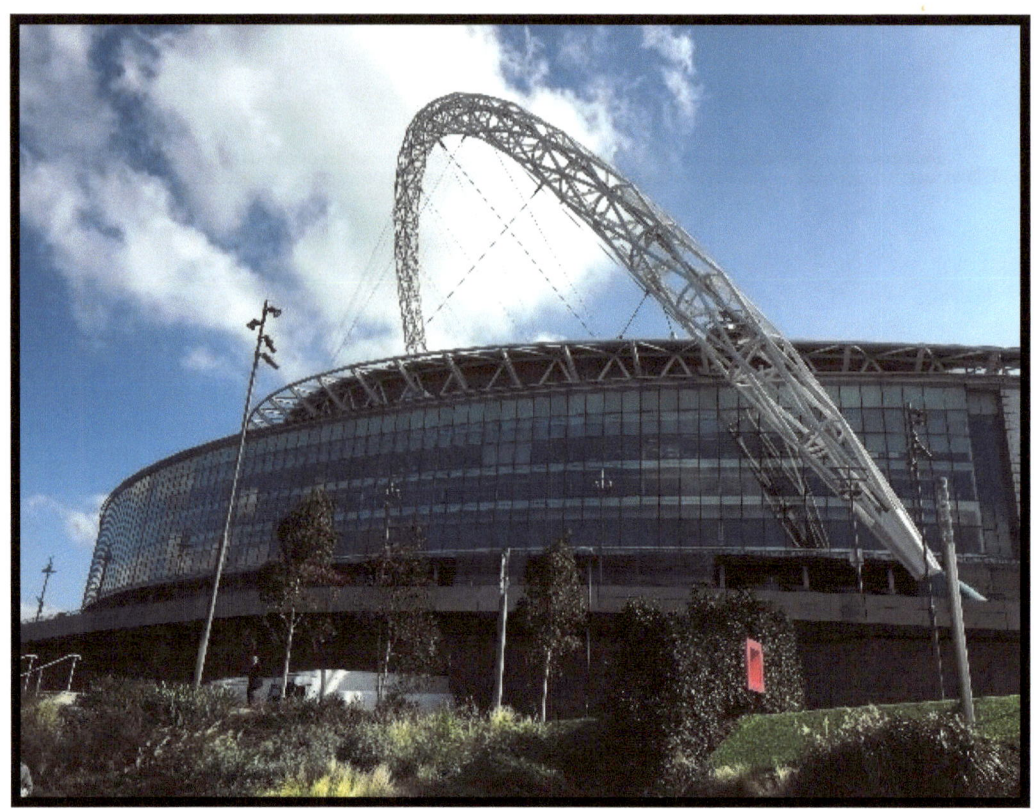

London HA9 0WS

Wembley Stadium hosts major football matches, including the FA Cup Final. It holds all the home matches of the England team. A statue of Bobby Moore, the 1966 World Cup winning Captain, stands outside the entrance. It can hold major concerts and bands such as Oasis, Foo Fighters, The Killers and Coldplay have all played there. It can also host other sporting events and Rugby League, Rugby Union, American Football and Boxing have all been held at the stadium. Nearest tube station is Wembley Park. Enjoy colouring.

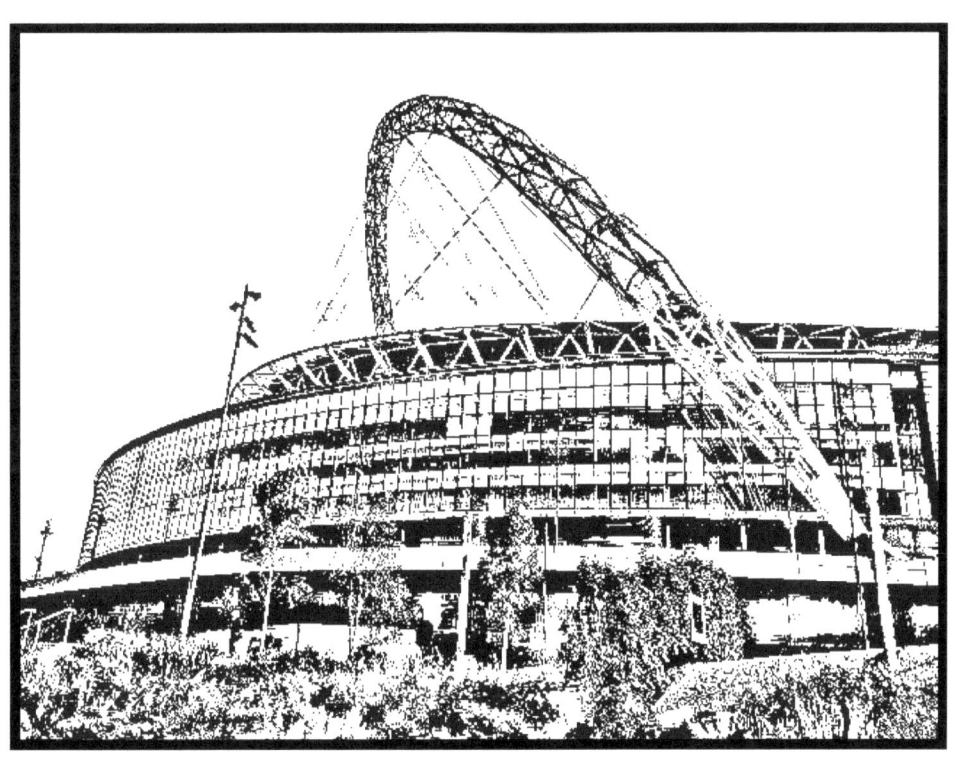

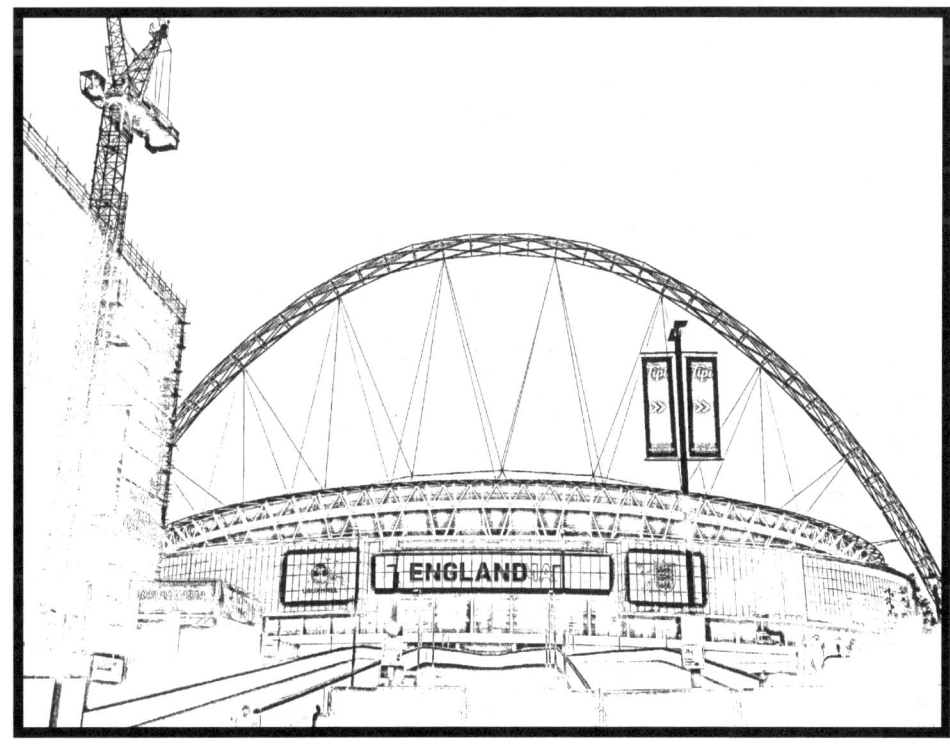

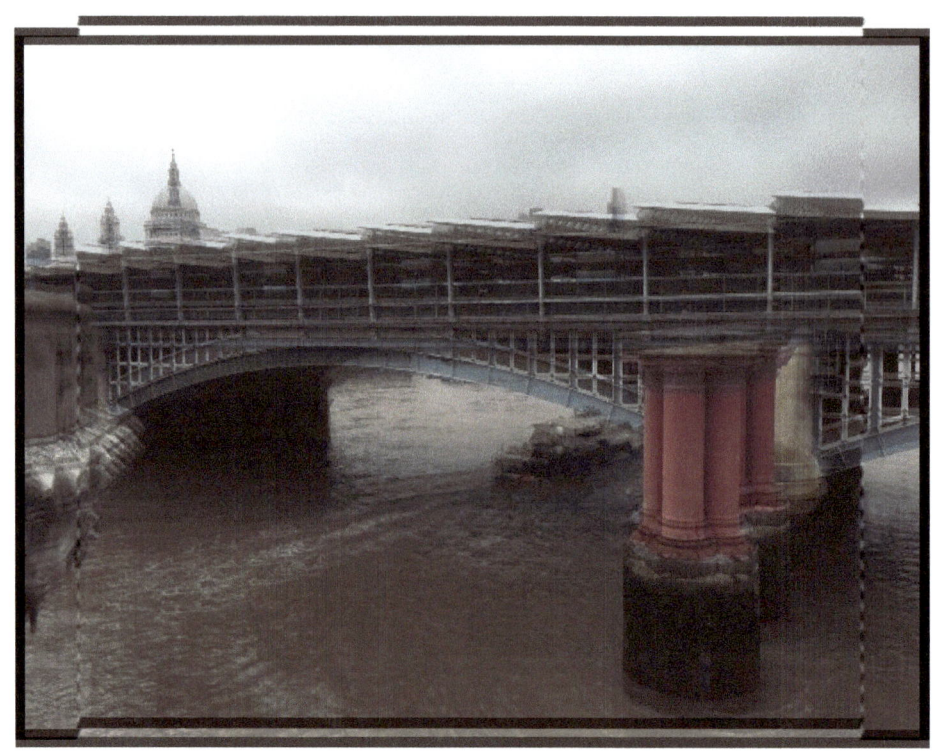

The River Thames, affectionately known as "Old Father Thames", flows through southern England, including London. It supports fish, birds and other wildlife. It is the longest river to flow in its entirety in England. In the London area there are over 200 bridges crossing the river, 27 tunnels, 6 ferries and a cable car. East of Central London there is a Flood Barrier built to prevent Greater London from being flooded by storms or exceptionally high tides. Enjoy colouring.

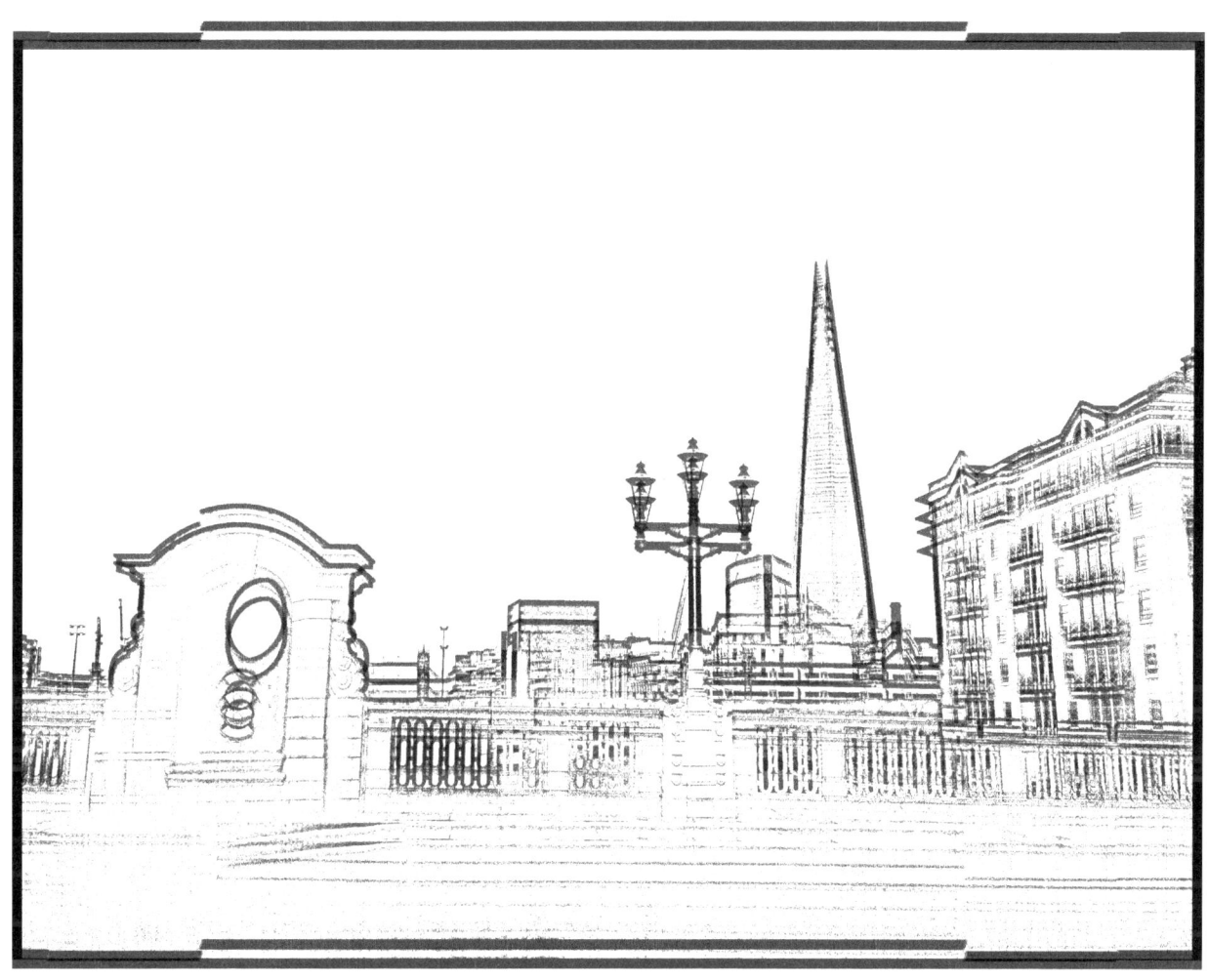

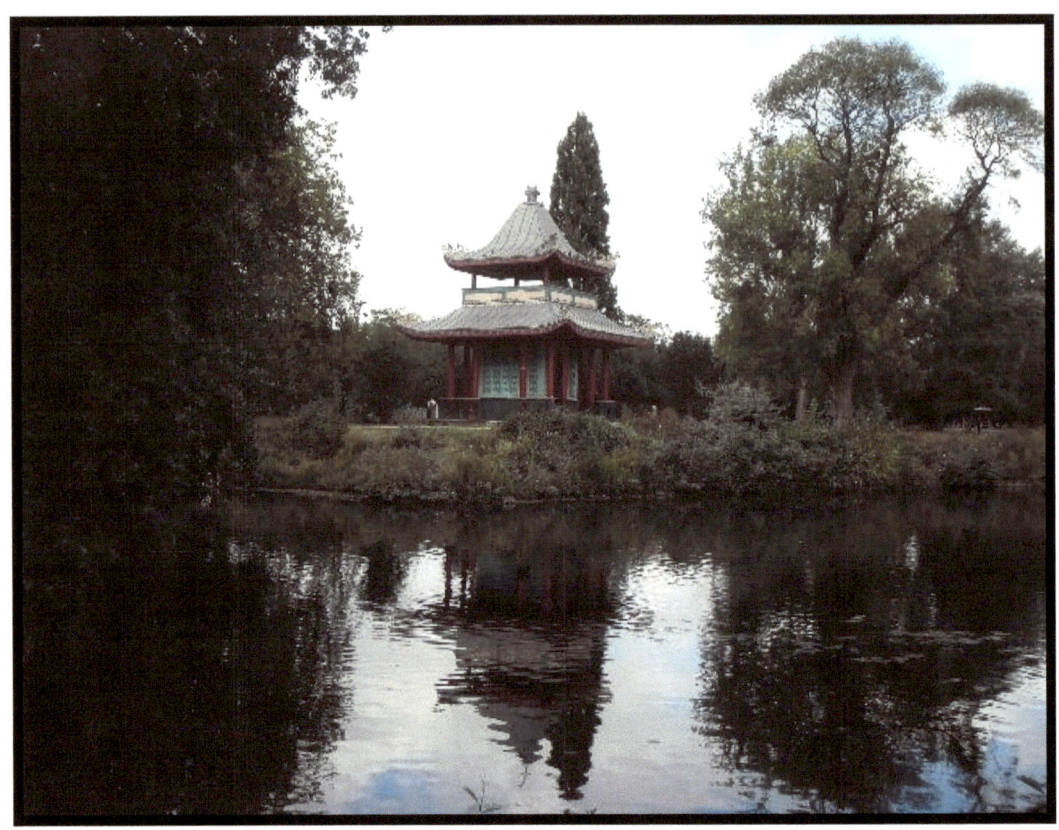

Green space in Central London consists of many small garden squares and eight Royal Parks. Forty seven per cent of London is green space and many people are asking for London to be made into a National Park. Many parks and open spaces are run by local boroughs or The National Trust. All are worth visiting. Enjoy colouring.

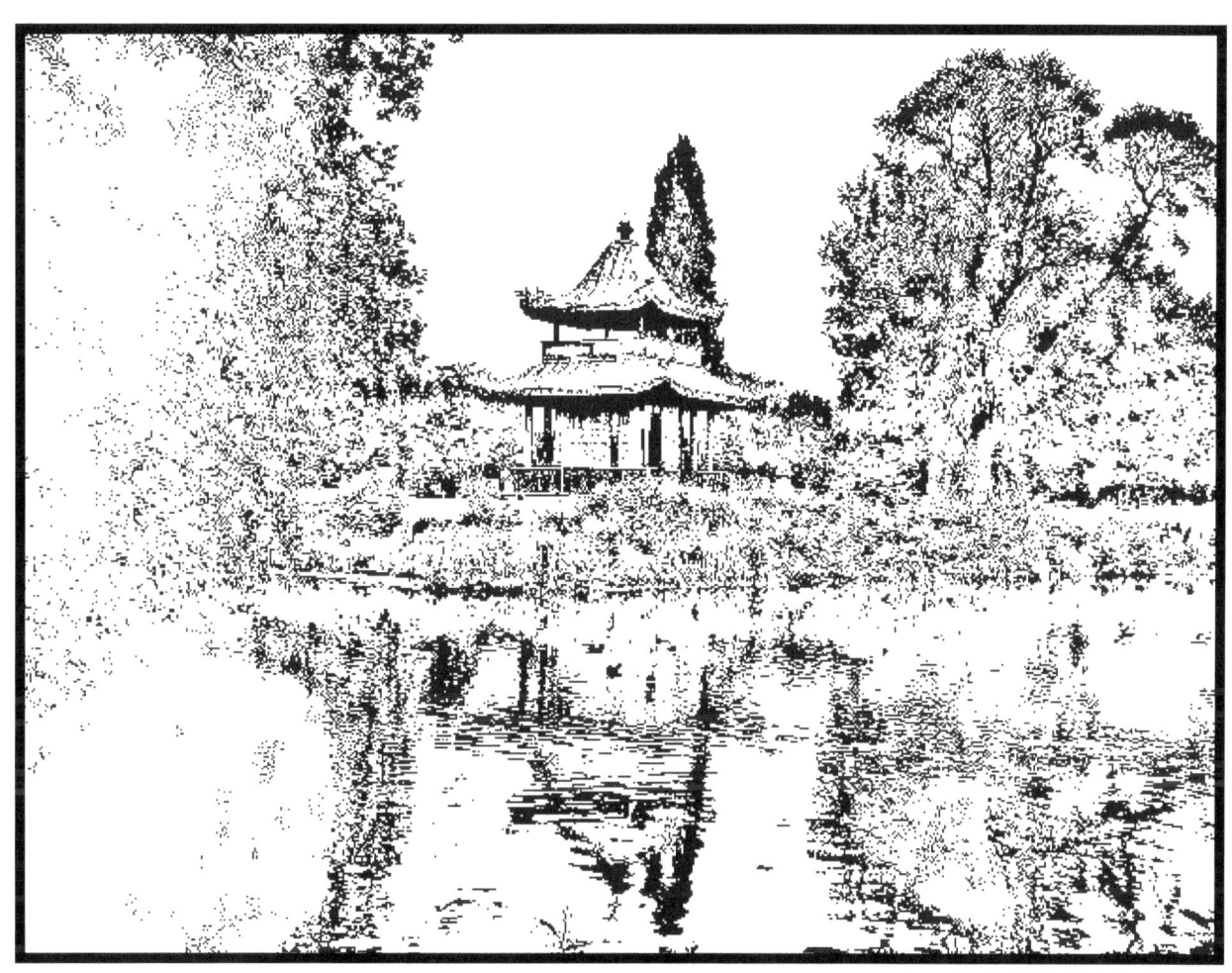

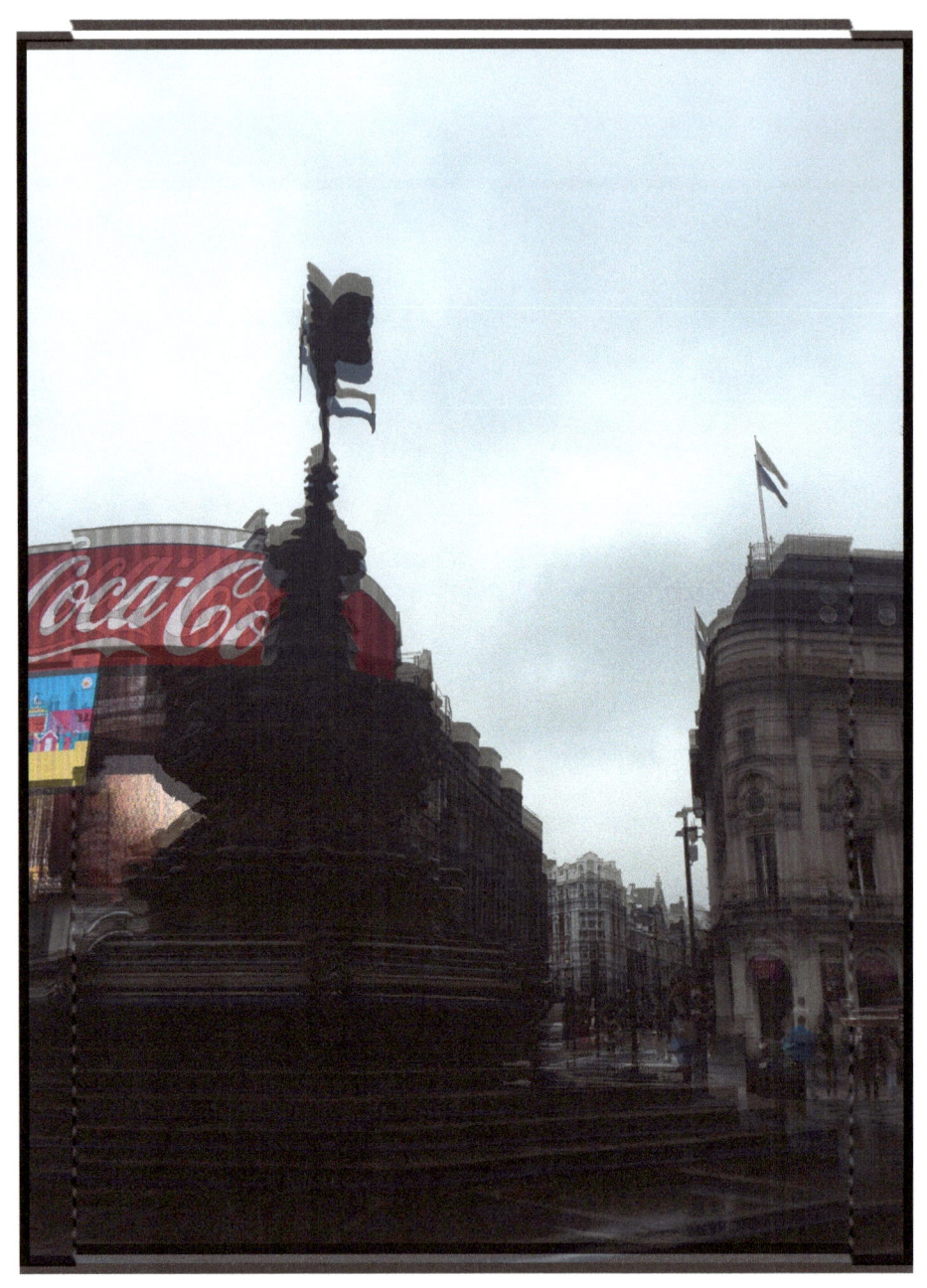

London W1J 9HP

Piccadilly Circus is a famous road junction connecting Regent's Street with Piccadilly. It is well known for its neon displays and for the statue, mistakenly believed to be Eros. Piccadilly Circus tube station is to be found underneath the Circus. Enjoy colouring.

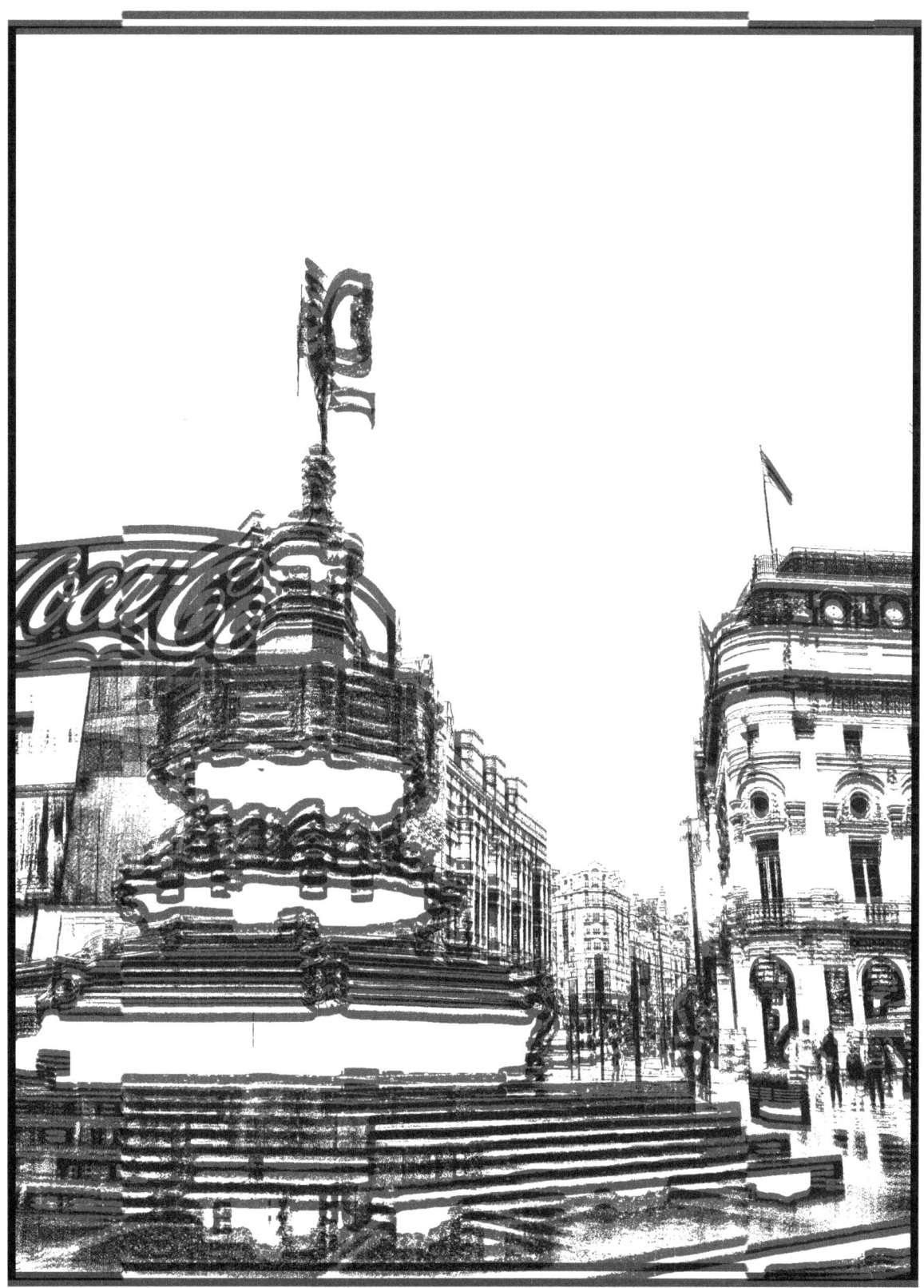

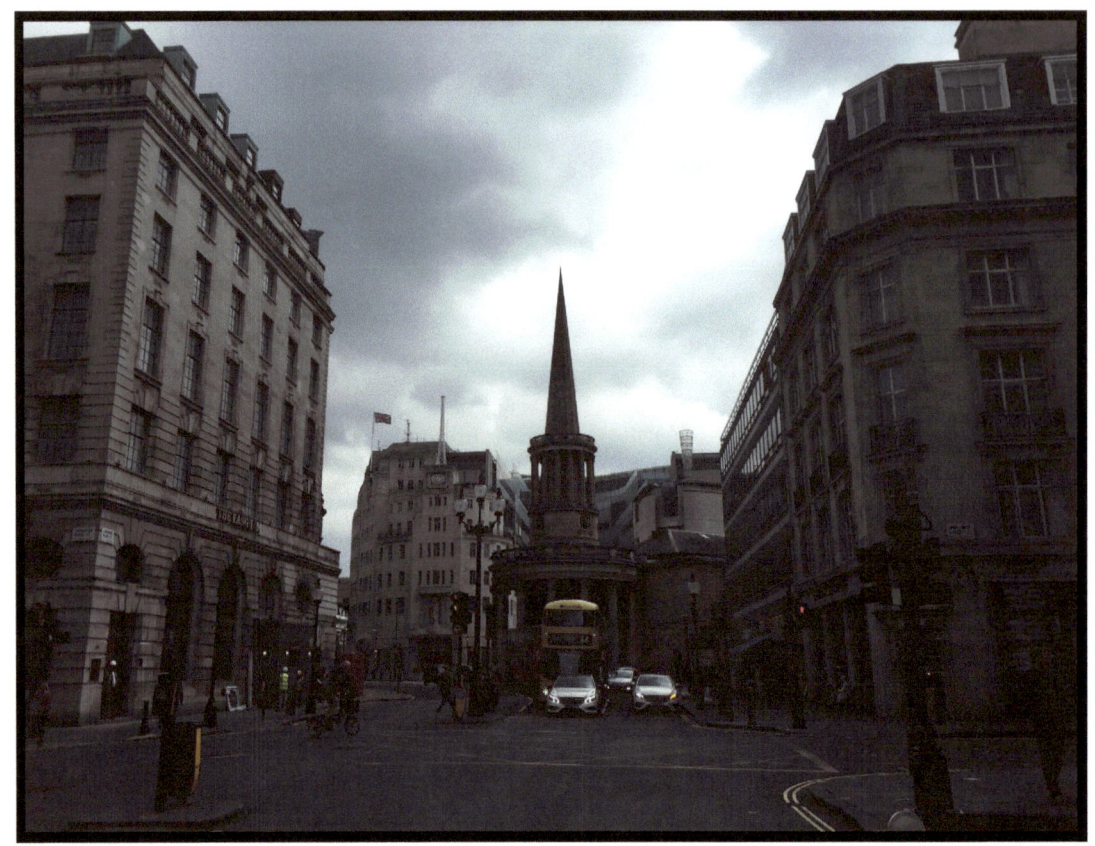

Regent Street runs from Piccadilly Circus to All Soul's Church. It was named after The Prince Regent who became King George IV. It has famous shops including Hamleys and Liberty. To the north is the BBC's headquarters, "Broadcasting House". The street has had Christmas lights every year since 1882. Enjoy colouring.

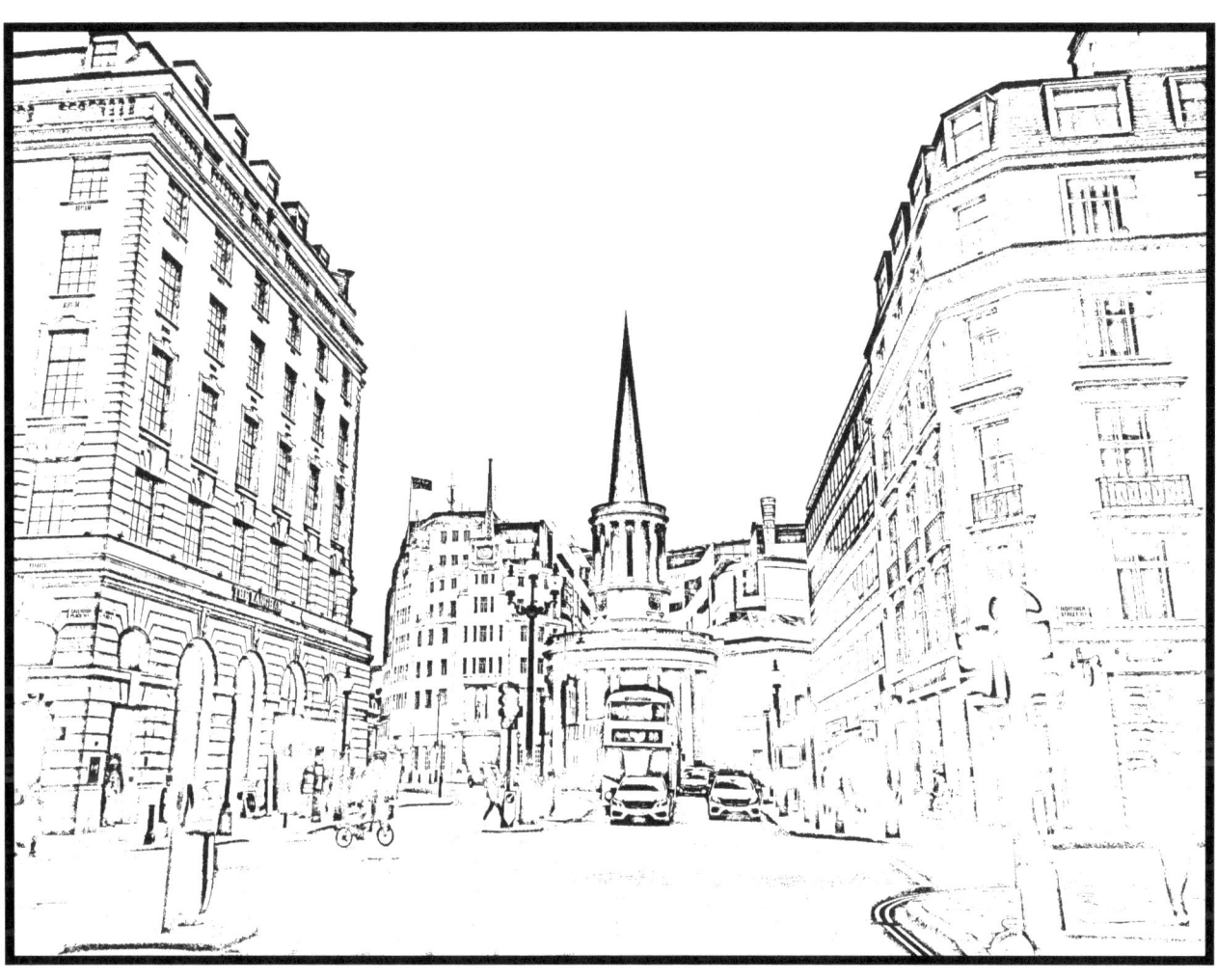

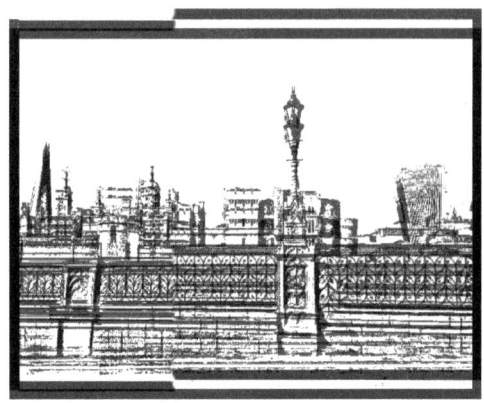
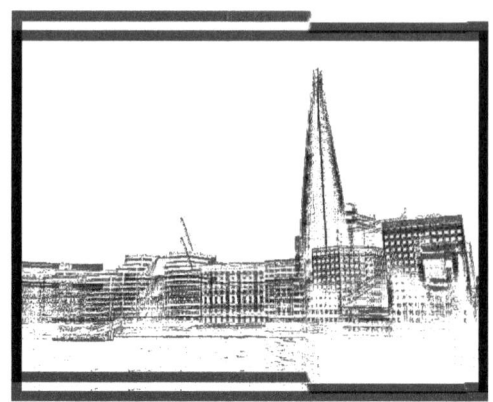

I hope that you have managed to visit most if not all of these famous landmarks. You will have dipped into the vibrancy, atmosphere and history of this amazing capital and will probably have realised that there is still so much more to explore. This is not a bland, grey city but quite the opposite. If you have the time then visit its museums, take a boat ride and walk through the parks and squares and amble alongside the miles of canals. You will be glad you did!

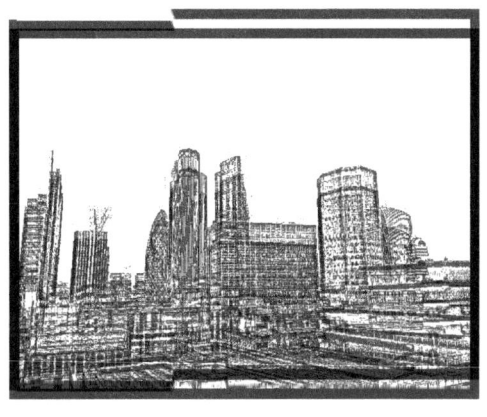
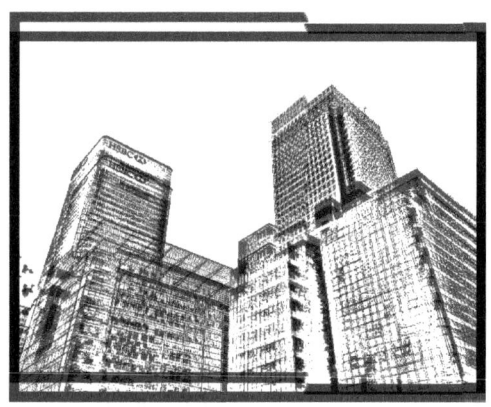

www.ingramcontent.com/pod-product-compliance
Lightning Source LLC
Chambersburg PA
CBHW051921210526
45473CB00006B/2096